"SHAKE YOUR LIFE"

IT WASN'T RAINING WHEN NOAH BUILT THE ARK, (not yet!)

(HOW TO DESIGN YOUR LIFE PROJECT
AND ACHIEVE YOUR DREAMS WHEN
YOU HAVE NO MONEY, NO SUPPORT
AND YOU ARE SCARED TO DEATH)

by ANDREAH SUCRE BELLO
April 2020.

WHAT IS THIS BOOK ABOUT?

Just when we are at bottom, we realize that the only way to continue is to go up. And there is no other option! ... The fucking options are over and that's because you cannot go down anymore! ...

It usually happens that, in the midst of despair or chaos, we find that ridiculous idea which makes us happy. And maybe it's ridiculous for others, but not for us, because IT MAKES US HAPPY.

My mother used to say *"people get creative in the midst of chaos."* I am the irrefutable proof of it, because I lost everything, LITERALLY. I have had to reinvent myself several times without success, because I lived taking into consideration the other's opinion (too much, I think). It was in the last reinvention I realized that only my opinion kept me awake at night and made me jump out of bed in the morning. I WAS IN CONTROL of what I wanted my life to be. I had two options at that time: to continue in chaos crying and regretting forever or grab my ridiculous ideas, and try to build a life where I was happy, no matters what, because nothing else mattered.

Last year, I lived in several countries where I didn't know anyone, where I didn't speak the language, where I didn't have much money and even so, I wrote two books that sell well on Amazon[1], I created a business from scratch that makes me smile every day (as sales grow) and I made friends who support me when I sabotage myself.

This book summarizes all the steps I learned in the midst of the blows, the gaps, the absolute and extreme negativity. This book is like fresh air when no one believes in you, not even yourself. If you are able to read it, and put into practice what you think can work for you, you will have taken the first step in building the greatest thing: "your life project".

Maybe you will not agree with all things I wrote, but who said that starting from scratch was easy? ... If you don't start today, you're throwing away another day and you're going to continue

[1] **"DATING WITH ME"** 30-days plan to become the person I would like to date and with whom I would like to fall in love; and **"DEAR PRINCESS**: No one is going to come to rescue you" Both written by me and for sale on amazon.com worldwide in digital and paper format.

floating in the current of life you've had to live or even much worse ... "helping someone else to build their dreams because you are not brave enough to work for yours; because you don't have what it takes to face life and say to yourself: "HERE I AM AND NOW, YOU WILL KNOW WHAT IS GOING TO BE GOOD ENOUGH."

Dare yourself to read the book; dare yourself to analyze it in detail, practice it and extract the juice. You can learn from everything. You don't even need to make the same mistakes because I already did them in advance, and I can teach you more or less the general path that will place you closer to the target. Write me a letter[2] when you feel this book helped you in some way (all kinds of criticism accepted, that's learning too). Remember: "everybody wants to go to heaven, but no one wants to die" ... and then ... how is it done?...

---

[2] andreahsucre@gmail.com

This book is dedicated to the evil friends who abandoned me in the midst of chaos. To those who told me that my ideas were too ridiculous and nobody would give me a dollar for my efforts. Also, to those who told me: *"stay with your husband, even if he cheats on you because that way you will at least have the money to live comfortably!"*

Mainly, this book is dedicated **to my friend MÓNICA,** who from the beginning and still without knowing me, believed in me, invested in me and every day, without any selfishness, enriches my learning process and makes me smile.

PROLOGUE

Many of us, regardless of whether we believe life has gone well or bad, or whether we believe we are happy or not; surely at some point in our journey, we will have asked these questions: What is life? and ... How can I live it and be happy? ... questions not easy to answer, for sure.

Some of us perhaps formulated them before, others later, others perhaps continue going through life as they were in trance and never allow themselves formulated the right questions. But among those who once did, a few may have already found the answers and they are applying them successfully day after day. Some others maybe keep looking those answers. Others maybe never going to be able to find them.

Meeting the author of this book has been one of the best personal experiences I ever had in terms of learning and satisfaction. She is a wonderful human being with a direct, casual and fun style, but always tender and gentle to speak. We have spent several nights of "long philosophical talks". We have tried, if not fix the world at all, at least to support ourselves to understand it better.

As a consequence, we understand ourselves better and this way, we try to answer together the initial questions of this prologue. Andreah's "philosophy of life" is very simple:

- "Do you want it?... go for it!
- "Do you like it?... that is satisfying you?" ... keep doing it!
- "Do you have an idea, a business plan or a project?" ... do it, but do it NOW!
- "Do you have a live?" ... well... start living it to the fullest!

Related to this way of seeing life, I remember someone asked me once (in a session of the diploma courses I teach) *"what does entrepreneurship mean?* and *what does it mean to be an entrepreneur?"*

Trying to answer those questions, first I obviously argued a bit of the theory involved in the subjects. As a project management professor, I explain to my students the origin of the entrepreneur word... "it comes from the French "*entrepreneur*", which means "pioneer"; and that, in turn, comes from Latin word "*in prendere*", which means "to take", initially used in the 15th century to refer to military leaders, mercenaries and adventurers who, like Christopher Columbus, "take the decision and the risk" of venturing into journeys, for which, they had any certainty about what they would find.

But, beyond theory, I tried to explain it to them through simple and everyday cases, saying, for example: "when you start a project or business, no matters if you are doing this for yourself or for others, you have an idea of what you wish to get as a result, however you don't have the certainty of what those results will ultimately be like, do you? "

Most of them nodded or answered me with a resounding "yes." I added: *"look at what theory is telling us: we can say all of us, who are dedicated to carrying out projects and that we don't have absolute certainty of the results that we will obtain, already we are entrepreneurs, right?"*

Likewise, in my intent of transferring this definition to our personal projects, we should say that every time we get up in the morning (most of the time without being aware of it), we are already entrepreneurs. Why? very easy, because we don't know for sure what will happen in the following hours, we don't know if we'll do well or bad at work or school, we don't know if we will finish everything we had planned, etc. And yet, despite all that uncertainty, every day we go out and do our best to make things go well, like every good entrepreneur.

The question is... Why when we consciously want to start something, a business, a new job, a new relationship or whatever; we feel that it costs us so much work? ... Why, if we are natural entrepreneurs every single day? It should be easy, but it's not for sure.

Perhaps the answer is we have never really become aware that we already are and we have so many and varied tools at hand to achieve this, and when we realize it, we are very pleasantly surprised.

Thus, considering life itself, with all the aspects that make it up as "a project", would it not be good then, if we learned (as much as possible) about how to undertake our life project in a better way?

That is precisely what this book does, trying to help those natural entrepreneurs we already are, take the leap, be aware, make up our minds and take charge of our life projects ¡as soon as possible!

This book, that more than a book is a chat among friends, a description of some of her most intimate feelings, fears, ideas and perceptions, about what we should all be doing to take, or resume, our project of life, which in the end, is the most important and valuable project ever.

In her prose, Andreah sends us a very clear message, from her woman's trench, to all women who, like her, have been through difficult times, or maybe not, anyway, it will surely be useful to them.

When I have read the book, I recognize that the ideas, suggestions and recipes of life, all of them full of joy, optimism and drive, aren't directly send only to women, but surely apply to everyone, men and women, young and old people, poor or rich ones. We all live, we all have (or should have) a life project. And we should all be very clear about our own "project plan".

No project is successfully completed without a plan. Our life project requires, then, a well-designed plan, it requires decision to start it ("having the balls", she says), it needs the best attitude and commitment to be resilient to execute it, and it requires, above all, humility to collect the fruits of our effort, learn and move forward successfully.

Thanks, Andreah, for showing us that you can, thanks for showing us that attitude is everything (or almost), thanks for showing us the way and, above all, thanks for sharing your way with us. Let's start together!

MARIO RIVERA CRUZ

CHAPTER 1
"YOUR PAST IS DONE"

I know, it's possible that all the bad things in the world have happened to you. It's possible that you are in the worst moment of your life because you lost everything and nobody invests in you even a free smile. And I also know that it's very unfair. But... Are you going to continue being paralyzed without taking responsibility for the decisions you made in the past and that probably brought you to this moment and place? ... Are you going to continue regretting and licking your wounds over and over, and over again, as if there was nothing else for what to live? ...

I haven't met anyone who can tell me that everything he or she has experienced has been good and that he or she has never had a panic or regret episode about his or her past. We are human beings and bad things happen to us, regardless of race, creed or nationality. Bad things are going to continue to happen to us so it's time to assume it. No one escapes the balance of life that sometimes is not so balanced at all. For me, for every good thing that happens to me, at least 3 things make me cry like a river. But this is simply learning.

This is evolution. Something positive can be drawn from everything, so believe me, this terrible moment will also pass.

The past cannot be changed. I invite you to make the exercise to try changing it. Try to do it! relive something you have done or have been done to you and try to go back to that moment and do something different. Did you see? ... you can't! ... and you can't because we don't have a time machine like we have a microwave oven. We still don't have access to that technology; perhaps in the future, as I like to think. So, what do you do remember again and again the bad things that happened to you in the past? ... does that bring you growth? ... quality of life? ... joy? ... money? I don't think so.

The only thing that happens when you relive the terrible past is feeling useless, unhappy with your life, ruining your present and remaining depressed about something that you no longer have control of. The only thing you can control is this moment; the decision that you are about to make now and which will build the foundations for a better future. Or worse still, a terrible future if you don't pay attention to the decision that you will take today.

The past three years have left me with a life lesson which I previously only took for granted. This life lesson is nothing other than being aware that the only important asset given to us with an expiration date is "time". We can lose the money and get it back, fall in love, suffer and lose our partner and find another love again. But time is given to you and never returns, no matter how much you cry or kick to have it again.

Your time is finite and we don't realize it until it's too late. Fortunately, when you learn to listen, the time you have left you learn to use it better and invest in you like never before. You are going to die, of course, but you will have consciously enjoyed your time. What a beautiful gift! ...

I used to assume time was infinite. That no matter what you did, the next day you would have one more day to waste. Since I lost everything, I learned every day counts. That if I didn't move my ass in the right direction, I was going to die starving or depressing. (Almost that it is better to die of hunger than of sadness).

But it was true. So many bad things happened to me that I kept complaining about my bad luck. I blamed everyone for my misfortunes; especially my ex-husband who, according to my opinion, was "the most motherfucker in the world", literally.

And the truth is that there are many worse men than him and since I assume my responsibility in this, I realize that no matter how bastard he was, I am the owner of my destiny and he was only a secondary figure in my project of lifetime. So, I took the reins of my life again and got the freedom of thought I was looking for. With this freedom came ideas, with these ideas came projects and dreams, and with them, it came self-confidence, satisfaction, success and, of course, money to my life.

What cost me the most was learning to live in the present. I was always a person who lived with half of the body in the future, always planning, always waiting for a miracle. I didn't realize that the miracle was me, and like the past, the future does not exist; the future is just an illusion. The present is the only thing that is, the only thing we can trust.

So, keep this in mind: "stop regretting, stop reliving the drama of your past, stop blaming others for what you didn't have, for what you suffered, for what they did to you and "take the bull for the horns!" ... so, use your time in the best way to create a new life. I tell you, all starts with an idea and from those ideas, projects are born. Stop wasting time with your head on something that can no longer be. Let go of what binds you ... in the end you have nothing more to lose, right?! ...

CHAPTER 2
THE ATTITUDE. "STUBBORN LIKE A MULE"

We are told since we were kids to have a better attitude. But who explained to us well what this is about? ... in my case, nobody. My parents and teachers always said ... *"have a good attitude"* but, what does this mean? ... smile when you don't want to? ... let yourself be cheated by others?... not to generate conflict even when you know you're right? ... not to cry when you die to do it, because it is not politically correct? ... I ask myself: *what is having a "good attitude"? ... where do you buy it? or where can you eat that?*

If we look in the dictionary for the meaning of "attitude", this is a definition to properly understand what we are talking about in general: *"a settled way of thinking or feeling about something"*

Simple, right? ... but not so simple.

For me, attitude is the basis of any entrepreneurship. It is the force which is generated within you that drives you to take one direction instead of another; not to give up when the odds are against you; to shake your butt when you just don't want to get out of bed and just want to cry.

I used to have a "very bad attitude". And when I say bad it is because my attitude was always directly related to perception and/or the benefit of pleasing others; which of course nullified me as a person. My attitude was not related to my purpose. My attitude was stuck in the dreams and projects of someone else: my ex-husband. And so, 20 years passed me.

It was very hard when I realize that in 20 years I did very little for myself; it sucks. You have no idea how enormously frustrated I am when I remember that I let literally a half of my life go by, waiting to realize that the protagonist of my stories, good or bad, is only me. I AM THE ONE WHO MUST LIVE MY LIFE AND SUPPORT MYSELF IN EVERY STUPID PROJECT I WANT TO DO. But, I couldn´t saw that.

This gives a lot of material to live in the past regretting or blaming my ex-husband for my misfortunes. And of course, he is a huge piece in my misfortunes, but I am also guilty of allowing it.

In the end, it's all a matter of attitude. Now, I can see things in a different way, thanks God.

Here, as I see it, I have two options: either I live in the past with a defeatist and miserable attitude, teasing my present every minute due to frustration and anger or I turn the page and smile, even if I don't feel like it and I direct my attitude to look for solutions to my problems.

That is why attitude is the foundation of everything. It is the first resolution to tackle a project. Because it depends on how you deal with the positive or the negative, and that's how you build the path to success.

You have to realize that nothing remains completely still. Everything will move forward and change, even if you resist or, even if you don't realize it. It will only depend on you and your attitude if you progress or stay in life that you don't like.

I changed my attitude after watching a TED talk on YouTube which changed my way of thinking (literally). And is that by chance the message I was looking for, came into my life to hit me in the middle of the eyes. One day, I was watching a video and YouTube literally "recommended" me to watch this one. (I talk about this in my first book, because it was completely crucial for me). It was as if this man had given that lecture to sit in the front row and beat me until ideas literally entered my brain. This man is called Victor Küppers and he gives a TED talk about attitude. He even proposes a formula to understand what it is about. As a result of that talk, I established my own formula to maximize the attitude towards life I wanted to have and believe me, without that, perhaps I wouldn´t be in the same place. I'm going to leave you a piece of what I wrote in the first book so you can understand how I conceive the attitude:

> "If I had to apply a formula right now that would fit me as God intended, I would say to change our reality, whatever it may be, you have to have the right motivation, you have to have a dream or goal, a written action plan (and serious one) and the "super attitude" to carry it out. So, since we are inventing "warm water" with the formulas which make us think, mine would look more or less like this: I introduce it to you ... $CR = (mc + s + pape)\, sa2$. I repeat it ... "the change in reality that you expect is equal to the right motivation plus a dream plus a written action plan multiplied by a super attitude squared".

It is overwhelming to start with something new, I know that. It is overwhelming to move your butt when you don't feel like it; when you have no hope.

And it is even more difficult when people who you love and care, hurts you, because they don't get it; they don't understand who you are or what you want to do with your life. Everyone thinks they have the right to tell you that if you want to start something, you must be smarter, have plenty of money and be trained, as if being an expert in something or learn something new are not for you because you are not good enough.

Starting a project, of course is difficult. And more if you have never tried before. Not only you must want it very much, have the resources and make a plan for yourself, sometimes you have to fight against all the negativity that people close to you; all those who tell you not to try, because your idea is very stupid.

When I decided to write my first book, (after crying six months on my bed and after my hair fell out), the few people who I told I wanted to write a book, they said to me that writing a book was a very stupid idea. They told me that a publisher and a publishing house were needed; Besides, I was nobody and there was nothing interesting in my story to have a viable project. They were very straight telling me I was a fashion designer and not a writer. That I was depressed and I needed to do something drastic in this moment of my life like getting a boyfriend to comfort me. (I never understood what the new boyfriend seems to be in this new project in which I just wanted to overcome the huge desire to keep crying on my bed).

The first days I believed all that negativity comments and I let myself be sabotaged by everything they told me. I felt stupid and became even more depressed. But after a week, I still felt the same desire to write and the fear of looking stupid seemed much smaller to me than the desire to do it.

So, I didn't say anything anymore and I sat for a whole month writing what my heart and brain told me was what I had to do. I struggled every second against the idea that "what I was doing was very stupid." At that time, I didn't care too much if I had no publisher, money or a publishing house to back me up. That's where attitude comes in and makes its move. I had seen the video of this man and understood that, if I wanted to do it and was willing to pay the price of the effort, then I should sit down and put "attitude" to my project. If others thought it was impossible or very stupid, my attitude would answer that "it was their problem." So, I did it. I was more important, for sure.

I realized the secret of success in people I admire the most are not only due the money they invested or their supernatural intelligence. I realized after long observation that the most important quality in a "winning attitude" is stubbornness.

It's that insignificant little voice that at first tells you: do it now! and that you feed every day so it becomes a monster and reminds you and forces you to move your butt when you had a bad day. The world belongs to people that are as stubborn as mules. People that despite the obstacles and the "it's not possible" of the people they love, they continue to do wonders little by little every time. And that's me now, the most stubborn of mules.

So many times, I have been told that I am not good enough to do things, that now if someone says to me ... "it's that you don't have enough money or knowledge" or *"it's that you are in a third world country"*, then I prepare more, I risk more, I become like a mule.

So, I read more books, I meet more people and I prepare myself in other languages. I have learned that every time I hear a "no" that wants to sabotage me, I put more desire into my project because it becomes an obsessive challenge for me to see if I am strong enough and stubborn enough to carry it out.

The negative charge now serves as fuel. I have become self-critical and dreamy in equal parts. My brain seems to expand itself at the word "no". Sometimes I am sleeping and my brain seems like never shut down, I find possible solutions (some very crazy) to things I want to do and I have no idea how to start.

The first step is of course BELIEVING WE CAN DO IT. When we come up with an idea that we are passionate about and even if the universe is against it (or at least that seems because it is not true). Believing that we can try it beside with the correct attitude is the basis of what will become an exciting project full of challenges and satisfactions.

You have to keep quiet the little voice (EGO) that manipulates you and that discourages you from the inside that can tell you that you are not good enough, that the idea is very stupid or that you have neither the money nor the skills to carry it out.

The first thing is to BELIEVE with the last cell of your mind and body that this is what you want to do. I promise you this, along the way, you will find the means and the people to help you carry it out. Start by believing it can be done, just do that!

CHAPTER 3
WHERE DO WE BUY THE IDEAS?...
AMAZON?

It is possible with some practice and experience to know where the new ideas are coming to your life. But it's not easy at first, when your self-esteem is badly hit or practically non-existent. Sometimes we believe that we are useless and that everything is made up. Sometimes, we simply believe that we are not smart or capable enough or we don't have the money to face that new idea or project. And yes, it may be so. There are people who are not very bright. There are people who are brilliant but have no drive. And there are people who are brilliant, have the right drive, but lack of resources.

In all those cases, you have to come up with a plan and find a way. Because there is ALWAYS a way, even if it takes us a while to discover it.

Ideas are everywhere and come to us in different ways. But most of us are going through life as sleepy beauties, envying what others have, what others do, what others have achieved and we don't stop to listen inside and out.

And that is the secret nobody tells you, that you must speak less and listen more. And it's not just listening to your friends or family, it's listening to everything, every sound of nature, every conversation in the middle of the restaurant where you went to eat. It is, above all, about sitting in silence and listening to your instincts or whatever you want to call them.

Ideas can come from a conversation you have with a friend. Lately, I have been letting them talk until they get tired and I just pay attention to them because I realize that I learn a lot even from the unjustified criticism and judgments that some people give.

Friends are an incredible source of ideas. The easiest, possibly. Because many have tried to do things that they have abandoned because they seem ridiculous, or because they took too long or because in the end, they discovered they didn't make them happy. And it's this "trial and error" your best education, because you already know what you are going to put into your project and where you certainly are not going to get involved.

I'm not talking about stealing ideas or anything like that. I'm talking about evaluating the attempts in different areas that have somehow formed your support and learning group in this life. And when something is not clear to me in the middle of the conversation, I ask the appropriate questions because it is very important for me to know why this or that did not work for them. This particular form of pseudo failure helps me a lot to understand what material we can be made of.

Ideas also come from the books you read. These ideas fascinate and excite me because in my head, I can capture an image at the convenience of what I think it's, and I am surprised when I develop it and it's even better. And neither is copying someone else's idea. Every time you read a book that inspires you to dream or become a better person, you are generating the energy you need for your brain to become a more creative brain. In the end, everything is inside you, whether you understand it or not.

People freeze when they think they can never have an original idea. I'm one of them. I always wanted something completely new to occur to me as a miracle, in order to say that I am the pioneer of this or that. And I'm still looking for my new idea. But, in the meantime, I develop other ideas that could be just as good as new ones.

We must understand that many things are already invented. Unless you risk creating new technology, almost everything has already been done for first time. What most people do, is really give it a new approach or refresh something that has already been tested several times with additional adjunctions.

This case forces you to improve it and try it again in search of new results. These days I went to lunch with a great friend who comes to Bogotá from time to time and he asks me: *"have you tried this new hamburger place in the city yet?"* ... I said *"no, but let's go eat there"*.

While we were on the way, my friend explained to me that some boys of about 25 years old, decided they wanted to enter in the hamburger business using the same ingredients that they would use at home, like making "homemade hamburgers". How many burger places could there be in this city? ... hundreds or thousands, maybe. Everyone likes junk food, and bigger franchises like Burger King or McDonald's or even El Corral are always full of people.

What would a 25 years old burger business entrepreneur think, who must take a miserable loan to set up a small shop and compete with such monsters in the junk food business? ... that is a completely madness! ... what is a crazy project and that the odds of making a name and prosper are against! ...

Well, these boys, with all sacrifice in the world, opened their small business with 3 plastic tables for their clients. They seasoned the meat just as they would at home, made their own sauces, and used butter to fry the French fries.

It was a burger which had already been tried thousands of times by thousands of different people, but these ones in particular tasted delicious. And the day we went to this place, we had to wait in line more than 20 minutes for them to take our order. And at least 15 more minutes to eat. So, the wait of more than half an hour was worth it; And I would go back to that place again, just to be able to taste the blessed fries, which made me to gain about 3 more kilos just by smelling them.

What I'm trying to explain is that these entrepreneurs did not invent "the fire". These boys wanted to do something and looked for the way to do the same thing that others had already done, but with a different component: "adding the plus of making them homemade". To make a long story short, these boys must already have today about 10 new burger restaurants in different well-located and expensive areas in Bogotá.

These entrepreneurs had a very crazy and possibly a very stupid idea. They had no resources and they came for a loan to start in a place where probably 12 people were a crowd. But ...their attitude was correct and they found a way to overcome obstacles and provide an additional component to what had already been created and tested thousands of times before.

I am never tired of telling my children how privileged they are to live in this moment; in this space and time in which with the help of a "click" you can learn what you want. And in 80% of cases (or maybe more), it's even free.

I think they don't know how much I have learned through the internet and from researching, reading, and watching videos of interesting people who have left me a lot of learning. Most of the young people of this generation, despite having everything, spend most of the time depressed, stalking lives of others, seeing what they posted this time, instead of concentrating on learning to be good at something new. It's as if they don't know the value of the great amount of knowledge that is available to everyone and that goes far beyond social networks.

It bothers me a lot when I hear one of my children say, *"mom, I am bored"* My first reaction is perplexity and it provokes me to hit them in the middle of the eyes with the first thing I find on hand to make them react.

How could they be bored in a house with a huge library full of books of all genres? with computers and unlimited internet connection to learn to speak other languages or to build something new? ...because that doesn't fit in my head. Sometimes I don't even want to go to sleep to avoid missing the tutorial that will teach me how to make soaps from natural ingredients that will leave me 10 years younger and more beautiful.

Ideas also pop up when you're looking for something and you find yourself with something

else you didn't even know you liked. This makes me smile because it happens to me frequently. Sometimes I am looking for information on how to remove fat stained jeans and I get tutorials on how to learn to make furniture. And I was amazed to see how 65-year-old women cut wood with tools that look like hilarious toys. And I dare to dream and start by making new cushions for my sofa.

I think it is easier when you already know in advance what you like. When I'm in a blocking moment, I try to look at myself as a child. I think when you are a child you are somehow clearer with what you dream of. I try to do the exercise of remembering what made me sleepless as a child. And there I sometimes find my ideas and answers. It's like magic. But, when you have no idea what you like, it's better to go into new things to discover what is that thing that awakens us inside.

For example, when I was living in Iceland last year, I was surrounded by extraordinary and well-known musicians. I literally went out with rock stars. The vibe was as fantastic as I discovered that I wanted to learn how to play a musical instrument. So, when I came back to Colombia, I checked my budget and realized that I couldn't buy a piano, but that I could learn to play the ukulele. And my budget was enough for that.

So, I researched online where I could buy one that was affordable and comfortable to learn; I saw a thousand tutorials for beginners and I even made a practice schedule to learn songs and dare to dream of the moment when my friends and I will be sitting on the sand of a beach, we would sing songs until we were voiceless.

Just thinking about it gave me the emotion and the strength to know that someday I would also learn to play the piano. When I return to Iceland I will no longer sit and watch them play and have fun... I will be part of them. And possibly, even people ask to me for autographs.

I like to think that human beings have a small bell and a thermometer inside that alerts us when something is appropriate for us. It doesn't matter how many people tell you that you can't or that you're stupid; when your bell is activated only you know what moves you inside. Maybe it's that you are passing a place or that you came in a taxi and heard a song. Perhaps it's that you overheard a conversation or saw a movie at the cinema. Sooner or later your hood will light up and make you vibrate with emotion at an idea, and the internal thermometer will confirm how much you want it depending on the heat it generates. And then, there is that you must be brave and think that no matter how you will achieve it, if you wish it, you will find the way. If you wish it really deep inside... "you will create your own homemade hamburger and take your project to 10 successful new places".

Desiring to have an idea and believing that it is possible, is fundamental here. Perhaps what you have always wanted is to learn some other language and talk to foreigners on trips to practice. Maybe you always wanted to be a fashion stylist, and change the life of a woman who is going through a terrible divorce, with a change of look. Perhaps what you always wanted was to travel the world and now that you are alone you can do it.

Maybe you don't have the money to start; maybe you have small children who you still have to take care of or maybe your job is crap and consumes all the time you have. But when you want to do something, believe me ... there are no high mountains that don't let you see the landscape. When you have discovered that thing which gives you instant joy, just by thinking about it, there is always a way to get there, even if you don't have any money.

I am not going to tell you that you will achieve everything the first week. No one can think that everything is achieved just by wanting it. I like to remind myself every day, just this: "A DREAM WITHOUT AN ACTION PLAN IS JUST AN ILLUSION".

I have to admit that sometimes I get mad at myself because I have no patience; because I despair of not getting the results when I want them. And I wish everything was as easy as saying, I want to do this and it appears as if by magic. I don't know if it has happened to others, but for me, everything I have proposed myself to achieve has cost me sweat and tears and many sleepless nights. The difference now, is that I work harder, because I believe that in proportion to the effort I put into my dreams, in the same measure the satisfactions will come. And believe me, I check this every day.

Now, I find inspiration in the most unexpected things. Sometimes I read emails from my friends who live in Switzerland or France and come up with new ideas that would never have occurred to me before. Other times, I go to the supermarket and see people in the vegetable area and something happens in my mind and I come up with new clothing or book projects. Even recipes to make at home. And I'm talking about small, everyday things, but it also applies to big life projects.

Also, it often happens that I want so much to develop a new idea and then nothing appears. It is as if my brain has dried up and the neurons no longer feel like colliding with each other. This can go on for weeks and gives me tremendous frustration and I don't want to do anything.

But in this path of reconstruction that I started a couple of years ago to build a new "me", I have learned to speak well to myself and to treat myself with affection, even when I want to hit up myself for being so brainless.

Now, my brain speaks to me beautifully and I forgive myself for not having all the answers, I take advantage of this time without ideas, to rest and enjoy simple things, like watching a good movie, eating a hamburger with enough calories or walking the dogs. And when I surrender to the idea that I have no idea, then as if I was living in a fucking movie, the fucking ideas I was missing start coming again. I breathe and laugh at the irony. It is part of the process. And as much as I want it, there is no magic formula. Not yet.

CHAPTER 4
"STOP SABOTAGING YOURSELF"

If I had known how to stop the sabotage years ago, today I would be in a very different place. Perhaps I would have felt better about myself many times; maybe I just wouldn't have turned 40 years old feeling like I wasted a lot of time. I guess after all, I had to learn this at the right time and that is all.

Because it was in "the loss" that I understood I was better without many people. As I said before, lamentations or complains are useless. Reflection is now what allows us to learn from mistakes.

Sometimes when I analyze my life, everything I did and what I stopped doing, I find a constant that makes me feel a little bad: "I lived my entire adult life allowing sabotage." And the sabotage came in 90% of the people I loved most in life, starting with my mother, my sister, my ex-husband and a very long list.

There are two factors in this sabotage equation that are indivisible and need to be well understood. The first factor is related to all those people you love, and who love you back, but who possibly sabotage you with things as simple as telling you that your ideas, plans and projects are stupid. Or that they advise you to dedicate yourself to something else because what you want is for people much more capable than you (or luckier). There are many, many forms of sabotage. The worst of them is manipulation, where my ex-husband won all the prizes.

The second factor in the sabotage equation is your inability to see this situation is occurring. It is realizing that even though your instincts tell you to do something, you stop doing it because what others think or how it affects them, is more important than what you think or want. This is your fault and your responsibility and it is time to assume it.

When you allow someone to impose their opinion over yours or make you change your plans because others seem stupid or unnecessary, then sabotage becomes evident and you must make a decision and action.

A "decision" to be able to find a way to handle properly how the little or nonexistent support they give you affects you, and the "action" of being strong to evaluate if what you want to do is viable and makes you happy. If it makes you happy, there is nothing more to analyze. You have to go for it and you have to take the world ahead if it is what is needed.

Sometimes people who love you and who you love back have no intention of hurting you. From their belief system, they can only offer you those behaviors. I have never thought that my own family wanted me not to progress. Or that they wished me not to be happy. But, when we are aware of the pattern of sabotage, we also have the skill to recognize that it is the only thing they can give, because they also have their own issues to solve in themselves.

And you have to be compassionate to forgive them and love them with their shortcomings. And more important than that, you have to temporarily remove them if they influence your decisions and projects because you are responsible for your own life. No matter how much they love you, no one can live for you.

Living with a strong and supportive family is very hard. You don't even have a place to go to cry when you feel like the world is falling in pieces and in front of you. But, there are all kinds of families, and certainly, the worst are the super toxic.

My family believed I was only making the wrong decisions. For years according to them, I must not have done a single thing well. I felt criticized even in the silent looks. The moment came when I didn't even feel comfortable in the same place and the minutes with them were endless. I just want to escape from them and from everything related to them.

With my "in-laws", the sabotage was of a different nature. "I was never enough", there was always a "but", "a stigma", "a negative label" that would not let me integrate to their "precious family". I was always "the witch", in other words. (Sometimes I laugh thinking I wish I was a witch. It would be great to have the power to prepare magic potions to rebuild some brains that only have a lot of garbage taking place. Other times, I imagine myself traveling on my broomstick to exotic places with pointy chic shoes).

So, you must identify the sabotage and stop it before more dreams you have die. At first, I tell you that it will not be easy and that it will make you cry, but as in everything, in practice there is excellence.

Listen to your instincts. Listen when your cells are jumping with excitement because what you want to do makes you vibrate. Those moments are rarely repeated and they should be enjoyed. If you can't do it without the people who affect you emotionally and who sabotage your dreams, at least have the courage to save your project for yourself and carry it out without others knowing. It will take more effort, but it is your decision and you must take the risks and hard work if you want to get somewhere.

CHAPTER 5
CHOOSE AND DECIDE

You must understand something very important: "everything you live now, everything you have now, good or bad, is the product of your choice and your past decisions". This is real. You chose a path and you followed it until today. Don't you sometimes wonder what would have happened if you had done this or that, instead of this? ...

Well, it happens. Everything you own or live now you created in the past. **This is the future of your present in the past.** So, it is very important to stop right here (in the "now) to choose and decide what will be the present of your future, if this can be understood.

A thought produces a feeling. Think about this. If, for example, you think money is bad and hard to get, you will immediately have a feeling of rejection of money. And with that feeling you will not take the necessary actions to achieve it. And this is happening with everything. If you believe that love only hurts, you will create a feeling of rejection towards love and your actions will be aimed at avoiding love no matter what.

Every day is a good time to choose among the best options we have. And everything starts from our way of thinking. It is a matter of sitting still for a few seconds, to see what our instincts tell us; if what is happening feels good or if the new path we should follow is convenient for us. We must remember that, in most cases, the answers to our questions are within ourselves and not outside.

When we don't decide, the most probable thing is that someone will take the decision for you. This is terrible. At the moment, you may not realize this great mistake of staying still, but with time, I can assure you, you'll feel a lot of anger against yourself, because you didn´t have the balls to take the decision that seemed most appropriate to you or your life.

Another thing that could happen is that sometimes we are in the middle with too many options in front of us and we feel overwhelmed thinking we'll not know which of these is the right one. The human being "always, always, always" wants to win them all.

It's like in those virtual dating sites where, when you see a photo of a man or a woman you like a lot or seems interesting to you, you still keep sliding the screen to see if there is anything better. In the end, you missed everything because you didn't make a viable choice that could stay with you. Well, pay attention to that old saying that goes... *"a bird in the hand is worth two in the bush"*

Indecision is terrible. It's a top spoiler. Making a decision and making a mistake is more important than staring at the ceiling waiting for a miracle to happen. The miracle is you. The miracle is the power of decision which you have when you make a choice.

When life gives you many options, even so, you will always lean towards one of them that you know will make you feel inner peace or will make you happy. It's possible that it is the craziest, the least thought, the risky one. I don't have all the answers. I only invite you to let yourself be carried a little more by what your intuition tells you. Only you own your own truth.

And, what happens if we choose wrong? ... and what happens if we make a mistake choosing? ... well, you will cry and you will learn for sure and possibly you'll become wiser and more successful.

And everything you learned won't be in vain because, next time, you will be better prepared than you ever were. And this is well worth the mistake, even if you don't see it now.

You will always have another chance to do better that time, no matter if it's somewhere else or with someone else. Many times, it happens that you chose a couple who broke your heart because he or she never loved you, while you loved him/her madly and you almost died trying to forget him. Well, thank and let it go because surely for your next relationship you will choose the one who is truly going to love you completely. Right now, you can't see it because your heart is broken, but everything happens and everything comes. And I am really convinced you needed this to learn something. Everything is going to pass. Believe me.

You will make stupid decisions with even stupider results. No one escapes that. But at the end of the stupidity you'll realize that you were practicing for what should really come into your life. If not, what is the purpose of life? ...wandering like zombies until everything is over? ...That would be very stupid.

I know a lot of people who are usually very hard on themselves. I have been my worst enemy for years, speaking very badly to myself, judging myself as if all the tragedies in the world were my fault, and besides, it took me a universe to find a way to forgive myself for all the mistakes I made and how blind I was many times.

You have to understand that everything is a matter of choice. If you choose to please others, you will never be happy. If you think you live a shitty life and you don't do anything to get out of there, you'll stay in the shit until you think about it again and change your choice.

If you want to start a new project, get organized, review the options you have and decide. Start by forgiving yourself for what you didn't do, didn't say, or didn't change. You can no longer do anything with what went away. Life is always going to put more options in front of you, whether you realize it or not.

So, better wake up and open your eyes because there is everything in front of you waiting to be discovered, seen and taken. Your reality is yours. Your choice is yours. The decision is yours.

I discovered through bad times that we are not in control of anything or anyone. Bad circumstances are coming, loves ones are leaving, businesses are falling, husbands are cheating on you, and toxic people are everywhere. This is to give you some examples, because many people do worse with terminal illnesses that they don't deserve or with serious accidents that leave them paraplegic and dependent on someone else.

We are only in control of the decisions we take; how we react to the damage that others do to us. Don't you want to grab and embrace the only control you have and which in the end, is the most powerful?...

Despite what you have been told all your life, the most important action is the one that leads us to decide. It doesn't matter if your decision was good or bad. Life will eventually will tell you if you were wrong or not and will leave you with an apprenticeship and perhaps, a great smile of triumph in your face. But choose and decide... and do it only for you, for what is right for you.

CHAPTER 6
COMMIT YOURSELF AND HAVE DISCIPLINE

Every time we start a project or plan we believe that the initial energy will last forever. That almost never happens. As the days go by, the routine, the tiredness, all that which not go as we would like, the frustration and even the dream, modify that initial energy.

We must be clear from the beginning what has motivated us to start with what we do today. Perhaps it's a feeling that moves you inside; perhaps it's a person; perhaps it's the financial reward that moves you. The reasons may be thousands, but find a powerful one. One that just thinking about it elevates you to a higher state of happiness and well-being.

Practice trying to remember what it feels like when you return to that moment; you're going to need it frequently when you feel like you don't feel like it, that you shouldn't have started with this that is killing you with so much effort and time.

I remember when I wanted to write a book and the only thing that happened in my life was crying and losing my hair. The power image of imagining myself on the cover and seeing me sign books at a wonderful book store, took me out of bed and put me down in front to my computer to start to write.

Every time I felt stupid or thought I had lost my mind, I went back to that image of myself, with my long curly red hair and my spectacular high heels signing books at a major book store ever. To be honest, I still have not achieved it, but that is yet to come, because I still want it and ask for so much, the Universe will surely say ... *"oh, shut up and take it!"*

Committing to yourself is not an easy task. You usually give yourself some licenses because "you have the permission to do it". So, you must take this commitment with a such seriousness you never knew; with a such purpose that is unshakable. It is not a game to look in the mirror and make a promise. It is the only way to respect this agreement you are making with yourself.

You are going to need to have character and discipline in quantities that you never thought you could produce. Because character is what keeps you determined when everything seems to go against it. Discipline is the act of doing the same thing routinely so at some point, it becomes part of your daily life, like an arm or a leg, as a reflex act; because discipline will force you to continue when you have terrible days of not being able to do it anymore.

I give you an example. I hated exercising all my life. For me to jump and lift weight in a gym was super boring. When I first put a foot in a gym, I was almost 40 years old. Since I was always in shape and had a nice body, I never worried about looking better or being healthier. But, in the midst of the Venezuelan crisis we were experiencing, we couldn't go anywhere and I wanted to have some "fun" with my daughter and we signed up for a gym in Caracas near home.

At first, I could not even with the treadmill, much less lifting weight. I had to promise my daughter I wouldn't leave the gym for 3 months. I mean, she gave me three months of commitment and attitude, because if not, I would have violated our agreement and she would be very upset with me. So, for 3 long months we would go to the gym 4 to 5 days per week. We started making a fool of ourselves because we didn't even have a routine. A coach helped us and so little by little we got to know the names of the machines, the muscles involved in the exercises and what things were better than others to advance in our purpose of looking and feeling better.

After a month, I felt that when I had a lazy day, going to the gym made me feel better. After two months, my body literally asked me to go to the gym to workout. After three months, I looked at myself in the mirror and was proud of the small changes. I have been going to the gym for 3 years now with some intermittent periods where I have been living in other countries and the workout has been different, but I committed myself and created a discipline that has paid off.

I still don't like exercising, but it is part of my purpose, my routine and my way of life. And every time I look in the mirror, I realize every day is worth it. I like my appearance and I like the enormous amount of energy I am producing. All this, thanks to a promise I made to my daughter, but more importantly, a promise I made to myself.

Now I realize that self-discipline is even addictive. That when I have made up my mind to do something and I promise to take it to the end, staying committed has become addictive and comforting. Looking back and seeing how much or little I have advanced gives me a certain pleasure that I never thought was possible.

Another consequence of being committed and disciplined is that THE PLAN you have made, THE COMMITMENT you have given yourself, is what will get you out of bed when you are lost; when everything looks bad and you feel there is no hope anymore. **Imagine what a stubborn person can do with a plan! ...**

CHAPTER 7
COMFORTABLE ON YOUR OWN SKIN

Before facing something new, it's SUPER RECOMMENDABLE to be comfortable with ourselves in almost all aspects. That great truth is: you must love and accept yourself with everything you have. But, if you don't modify all those parts you don't like very much of yourself, that only will work for a while.

Of course, you must accept and love yourself as you are, because there is no other choice, I have always said. But there is a very fine line between resignation and change.

Human being, in general, and even more women, we believe that the most important thing is the physical part of our environment: our body, our car, our house, our clothes. Perhaps because in reality it's the first thing you can see.

But there is another part, that when "it's failing", it predisposes us even more, and it's everything we have inside and isn't easily perceived: our feelings, our emotions, our frustrations. We must pay close attention to this second category, because finally, it ends up impacting the exterior and although we believe that we look very beautiful, we will not radiate what it takes to really be beautiful. And I know, in the end, beauty is very relative.

I was one who didn't end accepting myself because I cared a lot about what others thought about me. If someone told me I was weighting extra pounds, I would stop eating for two or three days because of the anguish they made me feel. If someone said that my ideas did not sound very smart, immediately nothing came out of me and I spent days in absolute silence.

What makes you feel good in your own skin is knowing that everything you don't like about yourself can be improved.

Some people go through surgeries to improve themselves, others simply go to the gym. Some people need a life coach to guide them and others find refuge in prayer.

In the end you will not be able to grow the 10 cm you want because you can't, or you will not be able to develop Einstein's brain by reading two books. There are things that have to be accepted because they simply are not possible. But there is a lot more, "everyday ones", as I like to call them, which you can give a twist until you like them. So, for me it's possible to be more beautiful, skinnier, wiser, more compassionate, more patient.

You have to start with accepting where you are and the resources you have on hand to start anything. After identifying what is not making you feel comfortable, then you can create a plan to be closer to where you would like to go. Staying in acceptance is a mistake. We must work every day to be the best version of ourselves (inside and out). And this is not a game. It's a fucking job that will leave you exhausted.

I grew up with a very demanding mother, with such high standards that you had to work hard to win her approval. My mom put all her pressure on me and by the time my sister was born, she had the Sonia´s most relaxed part. I think I do the same with my children, although with a little less intensity because now, I can identify the balance we need.

My mother used to tell me that I should be "good at everything", but for me "that good at everything" means "perfect at everything". So, when I was little and I did athletics at school, it was super important for me to win the competitions. When I learned to swim and was part of a swim team, I must also be the best and I swam until I had leg cramps.

When my mother taught us how to cook, I achieved such a degree of concentration that, just by watching her cooking, I had already developed an improved technique; and I was only a 12 years old girl!... do you have any idea what pressure this is for a 12 years old girl? ...

As you grow and continue to nurture the idea that you must be "the best at everything," the challenges continue to be uphill. At school, you must be the most popular, at university you must be the most intelligent, the one who gives the graduation speech. There is a long list of things you need to excel at to fit in where you are supposed to.

Over the years, with the trips, the books, the successful people I met, especially in the last 3 years, I DISCOVERED as if it had been the best kept secret in the world and only for privileged people, that what you really should do is to be good at something you are passionate about; that thing or activity which takes away your sleep and what you would do even if nobody didn't pay you a dollar. Now, this is my phrase of the day and I put them in my children's heads until they are literally fed up. And I think it is working.

Each one of us has a skill inside, a good one, I have no doubt. There are many who discover it when they are 10 years old and others who don't know it until after 40. But seriously, it's true, that we can all stand out in something.

When I was studying the first semester of Fashion Design in Caracas, I had a teacher who was a recent graduate. Apparently, she was pretty good at what she had learned.

One day, I asked her if she believes I would do a good job in the future and she only asked me: *"do you love it? are you going to be happy with the result?"* there, I found my answer.

I was making a big effort to pay for the design school and I had two little children waiting for me at home. I had to go through a previous career in languages to get there. I had to argue day and night with my ex-husband in order to study again at this university because it was extremely expensive and he didn't want to help.

I had to take care of a house, two small children, two delicate dogs, a husband who didn't even know how to make his own coffee and on top of that, I had to prepare collections, sew all the pieces by myself and learn two languages in the same process. THERE WAS THE ANSWER.

This was my passion and that was my life. I wouldn't let anyone tell me that "I couldn't do it, not even for money". And for 3 years I went every afternoon to my university to study fashion design, and I came home almost dying of fatigue to take care of my family, to take the dogs to the park for a walk, to deal with the stupidities of my ex-husband.

But the time passed and when the moment of graduation came, I gave my closing speech and obtained the medal in recognition of the *Summa Cum Laude* mention for obtaining the perfect scores throughout the career.

It didn't matter anymore about wanting to be good at everything according my mother's high expectations. My ex-husband's face didn't even matter when in the middle of the auditorium, he was surprised when I was called to the podium to give my speech to say thanks for the special mention I received and everyone stood up clapping non-stop.

All that work, I just did it for me, because I spent a life being good for others and trying to be perfect in everything when all I needed was to be perfect for myself, with all my imperfections.

What is about is choosing one thing, just one, or perhaps a couple of them that makes you happy, and putting all your attention and all your energy even if the world falls on you on them; even if nobody thinks you are good enough; even if you have another 500 responsibilities every day. Because whoever wants to do something finds time, finds money, finds the teacher, and whoever wants to receive miracles, finds God.

This wonderful teacher I told you about a few paragraphs above, I met her a few months after graduation and asked her what had happened to her work and career as a designer. She was super pretty and super happy.

I knew because someone had told me, she put aside everything that had to do with clothes and outfits and had dedicated herself to working in a hairdresser salon, because her dream was "to do hairstyles and professional makeup". I remember the friend who told me the story, she did it so with such mockery, as saying this woman had gone crazy and had abandoned a career to go to work as a hairdresser.

Well, when I met my former teacher and I saw her so happy, she told me: *"now I am doing what I love"*. And everything was in the right place with her, I could notice it. This dear friend and former teacher is called Johana Del Vecchio and she is a WONDER in her work. People make appointments days and days in advance so they can do their hair or makeup with her. She is no longer in Venezuela and works in Miami now. And every time I feel criticized because people disregard my work, I smile and say to myself ... *"I am a Johanna and I don't appreciate your opinions, anymore assholes!"*

Now you see, we have to find our passion, improve and learn as much as possible to "be the best at it" and stop worrying about wanting to cover everything. That is to feel good in our own skin because what we do makes us happy. Because we are so motivated that we want to improve every day. My mom used to say and I say to everyone ... *"when you find a job you would do even if nobody was seeing you and even if nobody paid you for that, and you get up every morning hoping to be able to do it ... there is yours."*

CHAPTER 8
AN IDEA - A PLAN - A COMMITMENT

We´ve already discussed it. You should have an idea of what you want to do. Something just thinking about it makes you smile like you were crazy. Something that makes you dream, that visualizes you there in that "here and now" that has not yet come, but will come if you have a plan.

All dreams at first seem too complicated like a huge challenge. Sometimes what makes us smile ends up mortifying us of not knowing how we're going to get there. And it's worse when you don't have money or resources, or people who give you "a little hand".

To many of us, it happens we believe we have a great idea and it can be possible with work and effort, and we end up abandoning it, because we see it being very "uphill" to make it work, because we don't have the money. It happens to me constantly. Only I have learned to trust more and trust I can achieve it with extra effort.

Of course, money is a great help and sometimes the basis of any project that is going to start. It still hasn't happened to me that I go to a fabric store and I say to the sales manager: *"I have a dream for a collection and I would like you lend me all the fabrics I need to design my new collection and I will pay you someday when I have the money back".* I really don't know if even designers like Giorgio Armani can do that; suddenly yes, but in the end, the store owner will want to receive his money back for all the fabrics Armani was using for his collections, for sure.

When I did fashion shows, everything came out of my pocket. Even from my ex-husband's pocket. And I spent so much that at the end of the event, you have to rethink whether it had been economically worth it. In my case the learning was always worth it. But that is a project in which you really need the money from the beginning and now, my efforts are directed to projects a little more flexible.

Today I am who I am thanks to "so much trial and error". So, if you have already identified what you would like to do with yourself or with a life, you should understand that although money is important, more important is your mental strength to carry it out.

Eventually the money will come into your hands, perhaps much less than you would like at first, but it will come, because money is a "moving resource".

To start, you need to be really clear about the idea. It must be so clear that you must be able to write in a multi-line paragraph all the purposes of your plan. It doesn't matter if your plan is small or big. It doesn't matter if what you want to start is a diet to lose weight or you want to open a chocolate store.

It all starts with a clear idea of what you want, what your expectations are and really knowing if you are capable of taking on this challenge. Over time, I have seen many people talk about their wonderful ideas with a passion that infects you someway and makes you move your butt off the seat. You hear them talk about their plans and strategies and you wonder if you hear yourself like that too.

But after a few minutes of conversation you realize they sabotage themselves with excuses, with things like *"I just don't have time now"* or *"I'm going to wait for the economy to improve"* or *"I'm going to start with this when my husband thinks this idea is a good one".*

It's then that I realize that although the idea and the plan are wonderful, those people are not committed to what they dream of and therefore, they don't have what it takes to get there with: "a stubbornness of steel to build habits and fight against chaos, in case they arise".

"An idea without a plan is just a dream". Dreaming is nice. I love to dream. But dreaming without going further won't get you ahead in what moves you inside. That is why you can dream but... "MAKE THE FUCKING PLAN".

You will wonder ... uh-huh! ... and how do we make this plan? Well, let's start with this...

1)   **YOUR IDEA MUST BE LOCATED IN A "TIME AND A SPACE" (Always).**

Let's take the simple example you weigh 100 kilos and want to lose about 30 ones, because according to your height it is what will help you to be healthier. (This is an example).

You dream with the top models in magazines, for example. You dream of having the body of your neighbor who looks fabulous in sportswear. You spend hours watching a lot of videos of workout exercises and healthy cooking recipes.

When you go shopping for clothes, the first thing you check is the store is sports and fitness section. When you go shopping for shoes, choosing sneakers is the order of the day. Well, there you have your idea: you want to lose 30 kilos. You know that despite being overweight, you don't have heart complications or hormonal problems. You know the problem is you eat a lot and live a sedentary life in front of the computer if you are at work, or in front of the television if you are at home. (This is scenario 1).

You may want to lose those 30 kilos but you have hormonal problems and also, playing soccer a thousand years ago, you injured your knee and now you can't even go up the stairs because that causes pain. (Scenario 2).

If you are a person who wants to make a smart plan which minimizes the process of "trial and error", you should really ask yourself where you are standing and under what conditions you are going to start this plan you are starting now.

It's very important to analyze where you are standing when making a plan. If you know you have a medical condition which does not allow you to do everything by yourself, the correct step is to make an appointment with the medical specialist who will give you a hand at their level of knowledge. It's possible that you will need help with a good diet that controls your hormonal problems, maybe some medication and even a physical therapist.

You cannot start this project by taking the responsibility to do everything blindly, because you could even make your condition worse. If you know you don't have major physical problems, then your plan might be to improve the quality of the food you eat, exercise, and drink more water instead of soda or sugar juices. All these factors you have to consider them from the start.

It will be the same with the time you give yourself to achieve it. Because this is where we must be realistic and not get frustrated. Sometimes things just take time because there is no other choice. Because the times are the times and we must go with them, period.

If you know you need to lose 30 kilos and that is the plan, of course, you are not going to lose them in a week. You could die if that happens. Do you want to die in a week because you didn't know how to make a realistic plan in which you can lose some kilos each week until you get your goal? ... (If the answer is you still want to lose 30 kilos in a week, then I will say you that at least you will die skinny. And at the funeral everyone will surely congratulate you on how skinny you died and how good you look at the coffin).

The correct thing would be to stipulate how much weight it is viable to lose each week by adjusting diet and exercise. And for this, you must set a goal and test it to see if it can be achieved. If, for example, in your goal you suggest that you want to lose 2 kilos per week and exercise 3 times a week ... after doing it for a week, you will be able to know if you were able with that goal or if, on the contrary, you lost 3 kilos instead of two.

This "trial and error method" will prepare you better for the next week where you will assess whether you will continue with the plan or need to make some adjustments.

To summarize these examples, I will tell you this, after the idea, you must make a viable plan where you achieve realistic objectives in a certain period of time.

You must know where you're standing to start, and what are the first things to do when you start your project. So, you will be able to plan a good starting strategy that minimizes the risk factors of starting again from the beginning. Realistic planning is essential to stipulate how long it will take you to do what you want. And you have to know that it's almost impossible to have absolute certainty that everything will happen in the time you wish.

Sometimes "over time" is that you will know "how long" your project will take. But if you don't start right now, "time" will continue to go without you, whether you realize that or not.

2)   WRITE YOUR PLAN DOWN, NOW!

Stop procrastinating or being lazy and start writing your ideas and your plan. There are people to whom you say ... "write your plan down" and they already abandon their ideas. How can this be possible? ... we are talking about your life project, your time, your happiness!!! ... and are you lazy to write a plan on a couple of pages? ... is that your future is not worth a writing exercise of a couple of hours? ...

Some people are so clear in what they want to achieve that they can get an idea and write their project as a first draft in

15 minutes. And it's that, perhaps they have already thought about it a lot and that was the decisive moment in which they stopped dreaming and finally made the decision. And I assure you those people are not like the majority of people. What is the difference between them and you? ... Simple ... they were not lazy to sit down and write their action plan with full details! ...

Just ask yourself right now, if you are too lazy to go for pen and paper to write a few lines. If the answer is yes, how the hell are you going to tackle a project of a couple of years at the moment when everything is faltering or you have to start again? ... my recommendation is ... put this book down and go to drink a coffee. You don't need to continue reading these stupid things I am telling you. Don't waste time! ... spend it watching TV! ...

3) CHECK YOUR SKILLS. INVESTIGATE THOSE WHO DID IT FIRST THAN YOU.

There is no longer an excuse to learn from the best. And everything is within a click. Even, we are in an era in which we can read anything through our phones. For example, my daughter no longer uses the computer.

My son Joan is starting a chocolate business. One day he said to me: "*mom, I would like to start a small business and I need your help*".

Of course, my heart was paralyzed with emotion. I had been telling him for years he was good at many things, but he always made excuses to undertake a project like this. It wasn't until I wasn't able to continue paying for college (because we moved to another country) that he understood that it was time to "move his butt in another direction, for his own good."

He told me one day, his dream was the cinema. I doubted it, because as a mother I have learned to identify weaknesses and strengths in my children as if I were a super power.

And I said, "*are you sure*? and he said to me: "*oh yes, cinema is my thing!*" ...
I never watched him watch a single tutorial to learn photography and film. The whole time, I saw him watching videos of how to make sweets or chocolate truffles. I knew that "the shots were coming". Her sister studies cooking and apparently, she is very good; just as my mother was.

But Joan, despite being determined to study cinema, did not spend more than a couple of days looking for information from universities that offer the career. And like all careers in which art is involved, they are very expensive. It would be a great challenge to pay for a scholarship that in the end would not give my son the fullness he is looking for.

Since I have known my children (that is, of course, all my life), I always knew their inclinations were directed towards art like me, and not towards engineering and mathematics like their father. This was a big problem for years. Their father always made them feel that their inclinations denigrated them and they were not enough. It took my daughter over a year to tell her dad she wanted to study cooking. Of course, his father didn't take it well and it was another 6 months of arguing until he relented after many of my yelling.

My son studied architecture in Venezuela. The only course that made him happy and took his sleep away was Design. In mathematics he stunk but he built models of "first-world urban projects". So, I always knew it and waited patiently for him to recognize which ones were his true desires.

One day Joan said to me: *"mom, do you think Orianna can teach me how to make chocolates?"* ... and I said: *"ask her for help!"*

Finally, my son understood his passion was creating chocolates, ganaches and fillings, and every time I see him make chocolates or cookies he is so happy, he spends hours in the kitchen like minutes. The work he is doing is so good, that he has surpassed his sister who was "the queen of chocolates". Now, they are starting to work together on this and I almost cry with excitement. My children have each found their way.

Another day, Joan said to me: *"I know what I want to do, but ... how do I start?"* ... the answer was there, so I said: *"look for info everywhere!"*.

My son spends an hour or two daily studying new recipes, new entrepreneurs, and looking at how much free or paid courses there are on chocolate masters. Religiously, he spends every single free moment reading, watching or talking to everyone who knows about chocolate techniques.

At least twice a week, he buys ingredients and tests fillings, ganaches, new flavors, and silhouettes. (I don't have to tell you that my son's chocolates are spectacular. I am so proud of his passion and effort you have no idea.)

Knowing who is doing what in the area you want to learn and try into is the foundation of everything. Thank God, there are great people who are not selfish with knowledge and are happy to share their successes and failures. (And it's true that it also happens that you get unscrupulous people, irresponsible or worse, lacking in talent and ethics that in the end, make your head worse than how you started). These people must be discarded and continue investigating. Because as I always say ... "you learn from everything" ...

There are people who ask me: "how long should I investigate?" That is a very personal question. There are people who don't even like to investigate. That seems stupid to me because the research is certain that you will make fewer mistakes. In research is the trial and error of others and there could even be the "new way of doing this or that" that you would like to approach to create a new style of your product or service.

When I was researching for my first book, I remember I spent about 3 or 4 months in which I just read others who had more or less the same topic of interest as me. I wanted to learn to communicate better, to know where to start, to have the tools to be more effective in the creation of a book than I had ever done before.

Now that I've created a fashion business, I spent at least 1 month evaluating my prospects and new clients, another month researching where the suppliers were, and a week evaluating only my competition.

You don't have to worry if your investigative process lasts a couple of months or a couple of weeks. Only you know how much information you need to feel safe and willing.

The only thing I am going to tell you is that no worthwhile research project can last 2 hours. You should consult all the sources you can, see all the videos or tutorials which will leave you an explanation or a new way of approaching this or that and you should, of course, search with the best in their field. We must always aspire to be the best in what we propose. And those who have already arrived are an excellent source of inspiration because they remind us that YOU CAN DO IT TOO.

CHAPTER 9
START WHERE YOU ARE
START WITH WHAT YOU HAVE

When I started my digital business, many people told me to better wait until I had more money to invest in professional digital help. I felt stupid because the only thing I knew about digital marketing was to upload photos on social networks.

So terrified of starting something on my own, I waited a couple of months to save some money and hire an "expert" to help me with the website, digital design, etc., etc. The "expert guy" did everything very badly. He couldn't even give me a decent logo for my brand even though, we talked to exhaustion. Then after paying him, he never fixed everything we talked before, so I didn't have money or a website to start, among other things.

I was depressed (and pissed off) for a week because I had no idea how I would do this again. I couldn't wait another two months. Sometimes you just trust in the knowledge of someone who knows more than you, and it just happens that the job doesn't work. Now it's time to solve.

In the midst of despair, I realized that I had to learn to do some things even if they were not in my area of expertise. I had no money to pay someone else. I could not afford to wait two or three months to start again. Technologically, I was terrible, because I was never interested in learning something that I could pay for. But this was a special moment in which I needed to move my ass forward no matters what, so I had to do it or die trying. Either I waited two more months to save the money or I started to learn how to do it. For me the use of time is very important, so the decision was obvious.

And I said before, you are only a click away from learning what you want. If what you need to do is learn how to make a web page, you will find the video which will teach you to do it; there are millions of tutorials that will explain you how to make web pages in a thousand different ways.

They may not be very functional at first, but with practice you will improve. And one tutorial will take you to another and that way you will know what works for you or not. There are a thousand of new approaches every day, all kinds of technical information; so, the most important skill you should adopt is learning to filter.

If after 10 minutes you realize you know more than the man or woman in the tutorial, just don't stop there and keep looking. If, on the contrary, the information is very dense and you can't even understand the first concept or explanation, breathe deeply and go back. If you think the information is very good, try again and watch the tutorial as many times as necessary.

Sometimes you just have to look at things twice to understand everything. Sometimes with three times, you remember everything and you realize there is "a lot of juice" there to squeeze out.

There are people who, for example, say to me: *"I am going to wait better to have the money to do this or that".* I used to be one of those people. Since I'm a bit stubborn because somehow, I got the money and eventually launched into the adventure. But I also discovered that when I was ready to go on an adventure, the perfect time had passed from waiting so long for the conditions to be in place.

Waiting for the money to arrive is a valid reason for some ones, why not? But, what if the money doesn't come soon and you lose enthusiasm or opportunity? ... What if you're using the money as an excuse because you're terrified of making a commitment to yourself to start something new? ...

Organization and patience are keys to start from where you are. To that, you must add a little research and enough mental strength to filter, so as not to give up when the first attempt turns out "upside down" and then, the stubbornness to stay just there until you succeed. Statistically, you will achieve it if you continue. It doesn't matter if you have to wait a year or ten, if you stay firm trying to develop your idea, in time you will succeed. Remember that old saying which says: *"even a blind donkey finds the well sometimes"* ...

I think it's essential to warn you about two important things: first one, you must start now (right here) and the second one, you must stop procrastinating. I never understood the word procrastination until now. It seemed to me the meaning was not clear or, most likely, the one who was not clear was me. And then I understood that when you procrastinate, what you do is delay what you have to do out of fear or laziness. It's when, although you know what the next steps to follow are, you take care of something else to postpone what in principle you don't know how to face, for whatever reason.

For me, procrastination is ugly and I was the princess of procrastination for years and years until the need to get ahead in the midst of chaos put me in the only possible position: move my butt and stop delaying what I had to do.

Let's do it. Have the strength to keep your plan to yourself or to discuss it with the right people you know will not put you off.

I had just arrived from Iceland and had to live again in Colombia and that made me feel a little lost again. I had left my soul on that island, with all my work plans too and now, I was back in the third world and with little money to face a new project.

It happened to me once, I had the idea of telling my business plan to a friend and I ended up so discouraged that I tried not to think about my business plan for a month of how lack of wisdom I felt.

It seemed to me that a person like him, whom I consider quite successful, could be right and I did not even dare to continue considering my plans for days. That was a huge mistake. Nobody has the right to kill your plans with an opinion.

My idea was still there and I decided to try it even with the opinion of my smart friends, so one day I was going through a fabric store and I bought the most beautiful fabrics I could find to make myself exclusive clothes to go to the gym.

I started making patterns, taking risks with colors and shapes and I thought for a few seconds if these clothes were comfortable and made me happy, at least I would try it for myself and have a lot of fun in the process.

The first week, I arrived at the gym in my new active workout clothing, I met my friend Monica. She was doing a class with me quite hard and she came to greet me and tell me that my clothes were amazing. Well, I told her I had made them all and we became friends from that moment on. Whenever we saw each other, I kept wearing one of my creations. They always seemed fantastic to her. Once we came walking back to our houses together and she said: *"you should make these outfits and sell them to the women in the gym; I'm sure everyone would buy some pieces like theses ones from you"*.

I could not believe it. A complete stranger had suggested me to do it without I could say a word, she had the same idea I had since I just came back to Latin America again. That make me smile like crazy and my dream was growing as well. But as always, my brain was sabotaging me with: "*it seems like a good idea, but I don't have the money to invest right now, so I will wait better to do it*".

Two weeks later Monica called me to say: "*be ready in 15 minutes! I am coming for you and we are going to go to the fabric store so you can compare them and see the prices*".

I said "yes", of course. When we got to that place, although it was not very large at all, I found about 70 percent of everything I needed to get started and at fairly reasonable prices. But, my capital budget at that time was quite modest, and I could not buy more than 10 cuts of fabric. Monica chose the fabrics with me and when we realized we had at least 25 cuts of fabric. While analyzing which ones I would take and which ones I would leave at the store, she told me: "*take them all, make these two designs for me and you pay me back when you sell half of what you did"*.

I must confess that my first reaction was fear. No one had ever invested on me, and also, I was a complete stranger for her. My ex-husband who was married to me for 21 years never said such a thing to me. My own sister who lived with me for at least 20 years also never supported me that way. I was so scared to accept the help and not being able to pay her back that I was tempted to say no. But she insisted and I took all the fabrics.

The commitment I had made would surely not let me sleep for three days. So it was. But the next morning I woke up at 6, I organized all the designs and patterns I wanted to make and I made Monica two leggings pants to go to work out. She looked gorgeous. The outfits were ready and now I had to sell them to be able to pay Monica back that amount of money which seemed to me very difficult to pay at that moment.

On top of everything, December season was coming and Bogotá was empty. It was not a good season to start selling gym clothing when everybody is going out of city to spend time with their love ones in other places.

So, I had to add to this the thousands of expenses that would come with the season. I was scared to death. However, one day I left with my freshly made outfit for the gym and started offering it to my classmates. The success was resounding from the beginning. The few people who were still working out with us were interested in my clothes and I couldn't believe it. (You should know in this city they all look like vampires; nobody comes out of the black pants. And they were buying colors!

Not only I did sell everything, I paid Monica the money back and although I didn't have much extra money left, I had left to reinvest in new fabrics and re-create a small collection again.

What I try to leave reflected here is something very important: **you must start where you are.** And the second most important thing: **you must** surround **yourself with people who believe in you and not discourage you with your ideas.** Sometimes angels appear in the darkest moments. Sometimes business-minded friends show up in your life because they know how to appreciate the quality of your product. Life takes you many things away but it also puts you in the right place with the right people who will help you in your growth; I have no doubt about this.

I would go so far as to say that now more than half of the clothes my friend Mónica wears for the gym are from my brand. And at least 45% of the gym class goes with one of my products. I am so happy, I can't believe it.

CHAPTER 10
LEARN HOW TO CHOOSE YOUR THOUGHTS IN THE THE SAME WAY YOU CHOOSE YOUR CLOTHING EVERY MORNING

My aunt María Elisa always used to say this and now I understand it better than ever: *"Sometimes it happens you hear it again and again and even if it's really important you never pay due attention"*. Well, with this advice, you really have to be very careful and pay attention.

Thoughts are powerful, as does the word itself. When you generate a thought, no matters if that thought is good or bad, in 80% of cases (perhaps more), this thought will become an affirmation or an idea. This idea will be transformed into an action.

How we perceive things is very important. Sometimes we don't even notice when perception is negative in ourselves. Sometimes it's not our fault at all, because some behaviors we inherited it from our parents, who for years brainwashed us.

Sometimes it's simply the accumulation of everything we experience and survive or our fears which have stayed with us for much time. These "thinking beliefs" (if we don't correct them in time) are only going to leave more and more negative and painful results in our lives.

I had found myself very negative and fearful all my life. And I had never realized it until my life began to fill with chaos. Because it turns out that when you are negative, because your thoughts are mostly negative, all your actions are usually reactive and not creative ones.

If you are always reacting or defensive in everyday situations, eventually the accumulation of all this will pay you off. It's terrible to spend a life reacting to everything that happens. And when I talk about "reacting" I mean we go through life defending ourselves from everything that happens to us, like defensively.

This usually happens to people who don't take actions, who don't create anything. And it also happens to people who always tend to think negative. Remember that your thoughts create your reality, whether you like it or not.

Learning to choose your thoughts in the same way you choose your clothes when you get up to go to work or leave the house, is not an easy task at first. But, as in everything, "practice makes perfection". It's a matter of being aware every time we have a negative thought.

How do I do it? ... have I stopped having negative thoughts? ... No, of course not. My head is always looking for a way to generate negative reactions to what happens to me. But the difference now is, every time I realize that I am thinking negatively at any situation that arises, I immediately shake my body and say to myself: *"everything will be fine, so breathe, Andreah!"*

I immediately feel calm and that helps me to be able to change my negative thinking into a positive one. This is not magic. It will not happen from one day to the next, as if you were able to change your reality like living in a fairy tale, where everyone is happy forever and ever.

But you must start creating the habit of responding differently to what happens; and, much more than reacting, you must begin to respond being in the best possible state: that one of creating.

There are many people you can read, who'll tell you the same. When I started looking for information to learn how to change my reality through the correct attitude, everyone seemed to agree on the same thing, but very few explained how it's done.

It seems to me that understand the technique is essential. Every time something happens to you and of course, you don't like what is happening, the first thing to do is to allow yourself to feel the fear or anger that situation produces in you.

Many will tell you that you should ignore everything and continue as if nothing. In my experience, if you don't allow yourself to internalize what's going on, at some point "these ghosts are going to come back for you."

So, understand what is happening to you. Take a moment to realize how you react to pain, despair, uncertainty, or fear. The second is to breathe. I would say that the first, the second, the third and even the thousandth, IS TO BREATHE. The power of breathing is pure magic. Breathing consciously and (with big puffs of air that you take in through your nose and exhale through your mouth), will give you a little momentary peace and allow your brain to oxygenate itself to think better next.

Then immediately look for a real or imaginary memory which has made you happy. Focus on that image or memory and for a few seconds just think about something you really like. I like thinking about a place I visited or a meal that left me with a huge smile. When I concentrate myself for a few seconds on thinking about something that pleases me, immediately the vibration I feel becomes alert. That way, I feel although what has just happened to me is terrible before my eyes, I will be able to face it.

Practically EVERYTHING can be faced, unless you are dying at that moment, and that, even if you don't like it, you are going to face it too.

Negative thoughts often come right afterward when you wonder whether or not you can handle what's happening. We imagine a thousand different situations of disaster, that we will not be able to achieve it, that it's so uphill our lives are going to be struggling. And it's here where we most need to be awared, that we are thinking negatively and we must know if it's better to surrender to what is happening or turn it around.

Sometimes you just have to give up on the situation because you can't change it. You must understand you're not in control and you can't go back in time to do something else. What you can do is react differently to the fact what is happening is just a stone in the road and now you must try differently.

When you get up in the morning and the first thing you think about is everything that went wrong the day before, or the week before or the month before, somehow you predispose yourself to that day also going wrong, because immediately your mood weakens and everything which happens through the day, you will not be able to face it with absolute objectivity.

There are people who help themselves praying, for example. Others meditate, others listen to positive podcasts to face the day (while they are dressing or eating breakfast). When I wake up and I know I will have a hard day (because I am in the middle of a problem) or I have not slept well from so much stress, that day I prepare the best breakfast I can make.

That day I watch some video on YouTube that talks about beautiful things while I get dressed. I don't allow myself to spend more than 30 minutes in a state of negativity. Now, I look for the tools that give me a break. I can no longer waste a day feeling sad; so, I try everything which works for me.

CHAPTER 11
YOU ARE THE STAR OF YOUR MOVIE

This statement cost me blood, sweat, and tears to apply and UNDERSTAND in my life. If you read my first two books you will have noticed that in my case, I was an extra in my own movie. And worse still, I treated the co protagonists of my own movie as "super stars" and they treated me back like a simple fanatic (in my own life).

Relearning that you are the star of your own life movie sometimes costs an extra effort, because you can't find it, because you don't know how to do it, because if you could, you would ask for "self-esteem in soft capsules" by Amazon.

It's very sad to live your own life without giving yourself the priority you deserve, valuing others as if they were better than you in every way. And it's possible that some stand out more than you, in various areas, but until you understand that you, with all your things, can become what you want, you will never be the protagonist of your own movie.

So, how do you imagine your movie is? ...

Can you imagine yourself as the dramatic and sad protagonist who is unable to do anything without help, because you are not good enough for something? ...

Can you imagine going from one place to another through life without control or direction because you don't know how to take control of your destiny? ...

Or on the contrary, when you think about how you would like the movie of your life to be ... do you see yourself smiling and beautiful doing what you like and making money with it? ...

Don't you see yourself in those beautiful shoes, walking down the avenue to get to the restaurant, where you will meet the man you love? ... or your friends who are crazy to see you? ...

Close your eyes and imagine the movie of your life in a year. Do you see something that tickles your belly? ... do you see only disaster and loneliness? ...

I don't think anyone with hope who is reading this book can close their eyes and see their film as a sequence of unfortunate events. I don't think so, although things seem to be very bad right now.

Try to see yourself in that special moment which brings out a smile in your face. If the imagination is free! ... If you could create the movie of your life right now ... who would you bring next to you as a co-star? ... where would you work? ... would you have your own business? ... how many kilos would you weigh? ... would you see yourself smiling going from one side to another? ... drinking cocktails and counting the money like the gangsters in the movies? ...

This book should be the starting point for you when you have not been able to start with what makes you smile like crazy but seems stupid. And therefore, this is the time to start working for the movie you want for your life in 6 months, or a year, or five.

Whether you like it or not, time will still pass. Whether you like it or not, the movie of your life will continue to roll, and only you will have the power to be the one on the front page all the time, or simply, those around you will see you and treat you like a simple fanatic. That is sad, that in your own film the others are main actors and you an extra.

It would be even sadder, with everything you've been through, you still can't raise your head to fight hard for what you always wanted. Today may be the first day of the new script being written. Take the cell phone and write a note with today's date and something that says: "*today is the first day in which I will be the protagonist of my life.*" Don't forget to set an alarm that reminds you in a year, where you were when you started. That is a great exercise.

I am writing this book and my alarm goes off. Exactly a year ago I was traveling to France - Switzerland for a season. Those days were the beginning of my adventure. Those days were decisive to position myself as the protagonist of my own movie. How many things did I not do for myself in one year! ...

I once read that the unconscious brain can´t really distinguish between a well-made visualization and reality. The sensations are so real that they produce emotions. These well-managed emotions can create realities.

Visualizing us in a year can be the beginning of your movie plan. Visualizing ourselves in longer time can take us further. In the end it seems to me that everything depends on the planning, the desire and the effort you put into it. It's about surrendering to the first ones, of becoming stubborn and being there despite the blows and hardships.

You will find everywhere "the path to success is full of stones". Sure, it's a terrible cliché, but very true. The path to success is not a straight line; according to how I see it, the way to success is a kick in the ass that can catapult you one more step or send you back to the starting point and without any hope.

I have found so many stones on my way to success, that I was always complaining and crying, but I stopped being frustrated and now, I have learned to build bridges, flying machines, clothing which makes me invisible, makeup to camouflage myself and thus, each stone works for my own purpose. Now, I am learning how to overcome the stones and how to be an athlete. I mean, I USE THE STONES IN MY FAVOR and this is a superpower.

Now, I finally understand that eventually and even if I have a billion stones left on the road, the real success is surviving them with the right attitude of learning and enjoying the journey. Many times ago, I was mortified to arrive to my destiny all the time and never payed attention on the road.

Now, I am less mortified because I have realized that as much as I was piss off I will not get there faster. What usually happens is that I stop a second for thinking in the right strategy to follow and like magic happens everything will keep moving.

The correct thought would be in my case ... *"I would not want to stay in this shitty place where I am, I want to go to a better place."*

By the way ... isn't that what you want too?

...

CHAPTER 12
"YOUR HAPPY (and SACRED) HOUR"

It should be MANDATORY from this moment on, getting "one hour" for you, every day. This hour you are going to give yourself every day is going to be your happy hour. It's going to be your sacred place to do what you want to do. And you are going to plan this time very well every night before each day.

I'm going to explain what is allowed in this hour and what is not, and you must make your own list of what you think should be done and what not, because in the end, we are all different with different needs and points of view.

So, let's define what "happy hour" means. The happy hour is going to be those 60 minutes in which you are going to give yourself a little pleasure each day, that only makes you happy, in the most selfish way possible. No matter how your day has gone or the thousand activities you still have to do, you will find that space of 60 minutes to give it to you, even if the world falls around you.

And since life is complicated most of the time, perhaps so that in the end you enjoy it properly, you should plan it from the night before. Remember that it's not just one hour a week. It's one hour each day and the main prerogative is that hour will be dedicated to something that makes you happy.

1) **One hour each day. An hour of 60 minutes and not 15.**

You should give yourself an hour each day with exactly 60 minutes. I know people who after 15 minutes decide their hour is over. Many think it's wasting time or feel guilty about having an hour of selfishness.
Don't make that mistake. Once you decide what you will do, then get down to business, plan ahead and give yourself the sixty minutes you deserve. And please, stop feeling guilty! ...

2) **Choose carefully.**

Choose daily what you would like to do in your happy, special and selfish hour. This should be planned with all the excitement of a first date, taking care of the details, looking for the best time and place. You are having an hour with yourself; the most important person in your life. So, think deeply about this.

3) Plan ahead of time not more than one day.

There are people who improvise wonderfully. In two seconds, they can create a fantastic idea which works out and is a lot of fun. There are others who, because of having long and exhausting jobs, or children and a husband, or exams at the university, are full of things all day and looking for a space is almost like an impossible task. Well, get organized and analyze the day you will have and find a gap of one hour. It doesn't matter if it's at noon or at night. That will be your time.

4) What makes you happy that you can do in an hour?

Many will say it's stupid to find something which makes you happy and only lasts an hour. There will always be someone who thinks that an hour is nothing to make you happy. But most of those who use this argument don't even have an hour a day to make them happy, because they are complaining about what they don't have. So yes, there are many things that can give you joy and happiness in one hour; things so simple that you would not believe how they can improve your quality of life.

5) These 60 minutes MUST NOT be used for something you know you have to do but don't enjoy.

It's not a free hour you will have to cover a need, such as taking clothes out of the dryer machine because they have three days there. Well no, at this time, you will not be allowed to do any activity you must do the rest of the day. This hour "must count" and for this, it should be devoted only to matters of pleasure or happiness.

6) Make a list of the activities that make you happy. Write it down and analyze it carefully.

You may have very little time to improvise. Possibly this seems very stupid to you. But it's completely necessary to make a list of the things that, being simple, make us very happy.

Does it make you happy to go to the hairdresser and get a hair style or a manicure? ... does it make you smile to sit down and read your favorite fashion magazine? ... go for a coffee and a piece of cake alone? ... draw? ... read the gossip column of the digital newspaper? ...

Have your list. Choose an activity you can do for an hour. Believe me that 60 minutes a day just for you, will be the best of gifts.

7) Don't you know what to do? ... What do successful people do?

I was curious to know what successful people do, to please themselves, even once a day. It seems that many agree in reading interesting books. I only found some few cases checking "social networks".

And it's that starting to find out the lives of others, often produces the opposite effect. So please, try as much as possible not to spend your 60 minutes on social media. Find yourself a deeper pleasure which leaves you with a rejoicing soul.

I also found that meditation is a great gift. Sometimes I give myself up to 30 minutes of meditation and when I finish, the rest of the day is very positive for me; It's as if everything fell into the right place. There are people who work on their hobbies because they really make them very happy. Hobbies like drawing, journaling, watching a movie, walking the dog in the park, going to a new pastry shop, watching a tutorial on a new recipe ... there are so many options to give us away every day!!!

We usually spend our whole day doing a thousand different tasks. Many times, 80% of these tasks are performed for someone else. Have you realized that? ... have you realized your time is being spent for others? to just earn the money you need to live, but you're not living a single hour to yourself? ... don't you think you deserve a selfish hour to be happy with you, even though the world is falling in parts around you?...

CHAPTER 13
READ UNTIL YOUR EYES FALL DOWN IN PIECES

There are people who say they don't like reading because it's boring. If only these people knew the competitive advantage of reading!...

I know a person who don't like to read, but who has finally admitted that thanks to conscious reading and the right books, his personal, intellectual and working world has completely changed. And now, he usually says reading is "the cornerstone of knowledge".

It's don't fit my mind that someone may not like to read. Reading is one of the great pleasures of life, which introduce you to worlds that maybe you didn't even think existed. It's a cheap and accessible pleasure which usually distinguishes you, in the proper way, from the rest of the people.

What I think about these individuals who don't read is at some point, they tried to do it and found the wrong book for them. Because it's true, there are books so boring or incomprehensible that you can almost (almost) hate reading. But stop reading forever? ... Oh no, no, no!

In case you don't like reading, you should know there will always be someone who is better prepared than you. And this isn't a matter of luck, it's a question of whether someone is willing to read, everything that seems to you a waste of time, you are immediately disqualifying yourself in the competition of knowledge.

Reading not only gives you knowledge, reading stimulates the imagination, problem solving and even self-esteem. Reading is so important that when the book is good, it seems the world freezes and you don't want to eat or sleep because you can't take it off.

It also allows you to communicate better with others, develop new topics of conversation, escape from reality and most importantly, it gives you the critical ability to recognize what can and can't serve to you.

When I was looking for common behaviors of successful people, (and I'm not just talking about millionaires and celebrities), I found that the people I admire the most are literally "book eaters" in different branches and specialties; even in those people who recognize that they don't like it very much, but who understand that knowledge is power.

I was always an avid reader thanks to my mother. Books gave me, in my childhood, the ability to travel to incredible worlds without setting a foot outside the house. When I was a teenager, I felt I was smarter among many of my friends and schoolmates, because it broadened my vision of the world and even made me "more interesting".

Already in adulthood and with a husband, children and some dogs, reading in my life decreased but I never abandoned it. Reading is part of my nights before sleeping, waiting for medical appointments or of any kind; reading is the most important thing when I wait in airports or when I go alone for a coffee and a piece of cake. Reading is something I do frequently at the time I give myself every day. And when I have more time, I can read for 4 or 5 continuous hours with the greatest pleasure.

Since there are digital tablets and the huge digital library of books of all kinds on the Internet, there is no longer an excuse not to read everything and everyone. And it's that digital books are so cheap, that even if you did not have someone to lend you one, there are always options at your fingertips.

Of course, I'm an old-fashioned reader who prefers to take the book and smell the paper. I am one of those who falls asleep hugging the book. But the digital option has been a great resource for me. Even reading has incredibly helped me to be better in the other two languages I speak, besides Spanish.

Every time I go to buy a book, I try to buy it in the foreign language and thus "kill two birds with one stone". Understand that if you want to be a better version of yourself, you should read until your eyes hurt. You must find the time and the book that will help you climb one more step in the process of your evolution as a human being and as an entrepreneur.

You must also understand you should not only read what you like, but risk learning new things that bring creativity and another vision to what you now want to learn. I always ask for book recommendations. Now, that I've been studying marketing and business, I ask who I think are on the right track about what they read. I always make a list of the next books I will buy and every time I finish one, I start another, almost immediately. There is a book that has considerably changed the way I view money, work, the projects I want to undertake and the vision of my future. This book was written by MJ de Marco and is called "*The Millionaire's Fastlane*".

This writer gets into your head and helps you rethink how you want to live, what works for you and why you keep waiting for the miracle when the miracle is you.

Other books that I have read or that I have in the list of future readings are for example:
- "*Rich Dad and Poor Dad*" by Robert Kiyosaki and Sharon Lechter
- "*The 4 hours Week*" by Timothy Ferris
- "*Think and Grow Rich*" by Napoleon Hill
- "*7 Habits of Highly Effective People*" by Stephen Covey
- "*The Power of Now*" by Eckhart Tolle

And dozens of other books, to write correctly, to cook and have fun, to have more patience and a better attitude, to daydream and a lot of literature

I read for simple infinite pleasure and among which I recommend these authors: Stephen King, Diana Gabaldon, Dan Brown, Isabel Allende, Margaret Mitchell, Randy Ingermanson, Anne Rice, Elizabeth Gilbert, Mario Luna.

So, I guess I'm missing a lot of people that I read and enjoy as the happiest woman on the planet. Read is a pleasure for me and sometimes I even don't know who reads the book until I finish it.

If reading is hard for you, you're going to have to get into the habit, because believe me, reading can be considered a super power. Not only I say it, those who know say it, those who reached their goals say it. If your problem is that reading is very annoying, start reading things about topics you are passionate about. Give the habit of reading a chance again. This can literally change your life.

CHAPTER 14
"YOU DON'T GIVE A DAWN" WHAT OTHERS THINK!

I will never tired of repeating this over and over again. I have already said on several occasions, I have spent a life, building my own life, thinking first of what others thought about me or everything I do. I did it for years and thanks God, (I stopped doing) what I could to make others happy, and so many times, not even I was happy.

That you don't give a damn about others, it's a superpower. Perhaps a top one on the list with stubbornness and planning. When you assume your identity and realize you are never going to please someone in his/her entirety, then you will understand it's a waste of time, energy and self-love to try to do it.

It took me years to learn my opinion is more important than anything. For me, my marriage was the most important thing in the world; making a decision without my ex-husband's approval was unthinkable. Many of the decisions I wanted to make, for example starting a new business, learning something new, helping others and so many other things, had to be filtered through his opinion. Of course, his opinion was always the same: *"now it isn't a good time Andreah, we better wait"*. And waiting, I waited more than 20 years.

Many people ask me: ... *how have you managed to be self-sufficient?...* that impression makes me laugh when I think about it.

I am not entirely self-sufficient. Sometimes, I think I'm not even a half self-sufficient. I think it was just, I have hit rock bottom so many times that even crying and desperate, I realized the only person responsible for my happiness is me and nobody else.

When at the end of despair, you realize you must learn to love yourself more, with your ugly or complicated parts, then it's that somehow you become self-sufficient for others.

You are never going to be entirely self-sufficient because we don't live on an island, we are not isolated from the world. According to me, being self-sufficient is a fantasy. I still need the love of my children, for example. Although I am not dating with anyone at the moment, sometimes

I would also like to have a stable relationship, which would give me regular sex, romantic memories, emotional support when I have one of those days when I'm tired of trying; and above all, complicity to start a project together that is very fun for us.

My desires to have all this, don't make me literally SELF-SUFFICIENT. But, since my children are already adults and have their own lives, I am not dating someone at the moment and since my new projects bring me upside down, I try to enjoy the journey with me.

I try to learn as much as I can and I have THE RIGHT MINDSET to fight for myself, for what I believe in and for what makes me smile as a stupid woman. Now, if I want to do something and it occurs to me to comment on it and someone comes up with a word that judges me or my idea, I don't become upset anymore. I breathe deeply and I don't say a word because I already know some people are really assholes.

Now, I look at the person who judged me with compassion and I try to hear why he/she is judging what I say. I pause for a moment to listen and analyze the pros and cons if there are any. Their opinion matters, only as additional information to avoid unnecessary failures, but it no longer counts to feel myself bad for having this idea.

That's why I like Monica. I don't think I've ever met someone to whom everything I say has the same answer: *"try it even if it goes wrong, Andreah. Maybe it doesn't even have to go wrong".*

I love when she says that. And it's not she always thinks that everything I say or plan is wonderful. Many times, she has told me: *"stop, because you are not seeing clearly"*. I also love that. Her opinion matters to me, but don't paralyze me. Probably, that is balance after all.

When I talk we have to give a shit what other people think, we can't go to extremes. The first thing we must accept is there are people who are more capable than us in various areas of knowledge and experience. That has immense value, because it's what allows us to learn from each other. If you are really smart then you know that listening is the key to minimizing mistakes; because certainly others may have already committed them. And we don't want to make the mistakes that were already made knowing how they are made, right? ...

Balance must be found in the importance of what others think. What you really should do and in my opinion is the most important, you should listen to everything but evaluate and make your own decisions based on two very important things: what you think about it and what you feel about it.

Tips are important. There are wise people in life who don't want to harm you. But in my experience, for each one of those, there are another hundred ones who only want to sabotage you, because in their own lives, they have not achieved what makes them vibrate and feel plenty enough. The few people I have met who are happy with their own achievements, with their lives, with the blows they have taken and with the path that leads them to their new goals, are not envious.

They would never tell you not to try this or that because they are jealous of your initiative. You just have to filter those people, I'm afraid, they are few, so, do this carefully.

When I was living in Iceland, I met one woman who is today one of my best friends. And believe me my list is super, super short. Anka is an amazing woman, born and raised in Sweden but married and living in Iceland for over 15 years.

She is a teacher at a school and lives in a town that probably has less than 300 inhabitants.

The town has about 3 or 4 streets and is in the north of Iceland. Aside from being a teacher and her husband literally a rock star, they live on a sheep farm. It's incredible the house they have on the edge of a hill, where every day you can see the sheep graze and the river move to its destination. We spent a couple of weeks together and we could talk about our business ideas. Anka is venturing into the business of sausages made from sheep meat.

When we were together, we exchange our business plans, more or less. We talked several hours about our ideas without selfishness. I gave her as much information as possible in order to add some strategies to start her new business. It was a lot of fun looking for the right name for the brand.

Now, I like to think that everything she has advanced, is also due to my loving advice to launch herself into the adventure of being a business woman.

Today, she is making spicy sausages and Icelanders love them, which isn't common in any way. What I am trying to explain is that it's very important to listen to others, but not to everyone. There are people who, even if they love you, and possibly love you a lot, are not able to give you good advices because they don't want you to make mistakes or because they really see your idea very difficult.

Others simply have no vision. Others simply sabotage you. And believe me, there are many people who love you, who are going to sabotage you. Sometimes they do this with intention, and sometimes without it.

Your skill should be aimed at knowing when another person's opinion can make you give up on a dream or project. You must be able to put aside the bad comment which dares to paralyze you and not let you start. That's when, knowing that you still want to do it, you must have the ability to give a damn about what other people think.

Learning how to listen to your instincts is very important. When you have reached that level in which you know and accept yourself, even with the parts you don't like and which you would

change immediately if you could (and you can);
then you know listening to your intuition is also a
superpower. Use that power and that the opinion
of others don´t prevail in what you know is for you.
Try to be fair, try not to harm anyone along the
way. No matter how you look at it, there will
always be someone who will feel offended.

CHAPTER 15
HAVE CREDIBILITY
HAVE A GOOD REPUTATION

Trusting in all you want to start as a project is the key. Not only the confidence in yourself, but even more delicate and important, is the confidence you inspiring to others.

We all live in a world of relationships where within a click we can send any type of information, good or bad. This is the era of digital business. If you are thinking about creating a business or taking your idea to a much more technological level, it's very important to work on credibility and reputation.

Eventually, if you are starting a business, you should know that it's essential to build a reputation; and believe me, you need a very good one.

I remember when I started with my digital store (Hope & Tails). The first advice I received was laying the foundations for a business where absolutely no one knew me: *"do the best job, be ethical always and the reputation and credibility will come alone".*

Many people believe that because the business is digital and nobody is looking to you directly in the eye or nobody knows you, you can afford to offer mediocre products. Don't do that, never be mediocre. In many cultures, but perhaps more marked in the Latin-American culture, we have the tendency to obtain the best with the least effort.

In Venezuela we always had a phrase to identify this phenomenon: "*be clever enough*". This means we want to obtain results without making any effort and at the same time, taking advantage of the occasion or the person (even both).

"*Be clever*" can sometimes work, yes, until you find yourself in the right situation which puts you in place and then everything falls apart.

"*Be clever enough*" in this sense is terrible. If you are going to offer a product, try to do always your best. The product you are offering should be based more on quality than on cost.

There's nothing more rewarding than when someone sends you a comment, saying "*excellent product*". Imagine the emotion you will feel, if someone recommends your product because it's very good.

I said this before, it's essential to study your competition. You will always get someone who inspires you to be better, to create better content, to raise the standards of your product. You will also get people who offer more or less the same product as you, and in that case, study the quality of their product.

It's in this case, where you are going to give your best to compete and take the credit. Not only are you going to sell more than the one who has a bad product, but you are going to locate yourself with those who lead the market according to the quality all of you are offering.

That is "choosing the winning side". The satisfaction of knowing you have offered a good service, a good product, or something that has given value to someone else's life. That is definitely priceless. Added to that, the money will start to flow and with the money you will grow where you want to grow.

So, when you are tired to work or you aren't inspired enough, look for rest and relaxation. Seek to do something amuses you and gives you a new energy. When we go through weird times in which we don't feel excited about something, the work we do seems to reflect that. For example, I have my days when I force myself to work and design something good and I don't have even a bit of inspiration. In those days, the results of my work aren't what I want and therefore, all that time that I spent forcing myself, turns out to be a waste of work, because the results aren't always the best.

Now, if I know that day, I can't create anything because my soul is in a moment of low inspiration, I take the day to relax and do something that I really like. The incredible thing is the next day, I am so inspired and calm that I usually work twice as hard. The results come out perfect just as I want them. Therefore, sometimes straying from reality is a great exercise in productivity.

Most of us feel pressured by the times and by the results. We have this idea in our heads we should "move our asses every day with or without desire". The pressure is usually so strong, that in order to do anything, we get a product that we don't like, because feeling the day was a day wasted, is worse than anything else and causes us feelings of guilt.

But, taking a day for resting and recharging energy, is it a wasted day? ... be honest with yourself. Recharging your energy when you have a bad day will never be a waste of time; on the contrary, it will make your next day more productive, and those great ideas that you usually have, are going to invade everything else.

CHAPTER 16
SURROUND YOURSELF WITH THE RIGTH PEOPLE
(ALWAYS BE SELECTIVE)

One of the things I usually say is "family is imposed on us". There are people who believe that we choose them before we are born in order to evolve in some area where "we are really screwed". Possibly yes, who knows! And sometimes, we have no choice and we need to live with that family who's in our life and that's all. Other times, the less, we feel blessed by them, because surely it could have been worse.

Regardless of whether your family has been imposed by God or by fate or you chose them (so in the next life you return to the source where you came from), we have been given an opportunity which very few seem to appreciate: we can choose our partners and friends.

Generally speaking, (unless you live in a country where your parents choose for you and that is the rule), we have full freedom in this era we are living, to choose who will walk the path with us. It's so wonderful to know we have that privilege! ... right?

Many times, it happens, that we choose people who we think will support us or make us happier and that is not every time the case. In time you realize that you have made a terrible mistake and that if you could, you would run away at full speed in another direction. But how many of us really run in another direction from the toxicity of those people we once chose and loved, and now nothing works anymore? ...

When I think about this and how we stay in situations which stop us and kill us a little every day, I realize we don't have the courage to get out of them. It hurts me to think that at some point in my life, I stayed, even though I wasn't happy, and I did the same over and over and over again.

Some of us wake up. Some of us, thank God, have a limit to continue living badly. But how many years do we throw away because we didn't make the most obvious decision? ...

Sometimes I see some of my friends and analyze their relationships. It usually happens to me that what I envied before from them, now makes me want to run away. Many of my friends live in relationships based on status, money, or comfort; and they prefer to get on with their life, floating in their shitty comfort zone.

You can see they aren't even happy at least half the time, and apparently, they don't care. They fill their days with food, obsession with perfect bodies and plastic surgeries, cheating to their husbands or wives and even getting so deeply into the lives of their children that they don't let them breathe.

And when I realize this, I am grateful I am alone and I now know how to distinguish the difference, between "being accompanied" and "being badly accompanied".

Children are important, yes, very important, it's the truth. But we don't even own the lives of our children. When we are parents, we've the responsibility and the pleasure of raising them to become good people. But in the end, they are going to leave the house to make their own lives, because they aren't our property.

Our sentimental partner should also be part of our priorities; our first person, our support, our precious, our partner, our love of life. Still, it doesn't belong to us either. He or she is an individual being who can love us or stop loving us at any time. We can´t control that either.

If we go back to the point where I assert that family is imposed on us, we could say that our children will be the result of genetics and chance. Perhaps then, they also chose us before birth to evolve. But we still have the power to choose our life partner, someone who will love us with our thousands of defects and deficiencies; someone who will stay, even when things get ugly.

I know, sometimes we fall in love and in the midst of falling in love we can´t see clearly how much that particular person suits us. And so, we throw ourselves into the abyss, with our hearts wide open, without measuring the consequences. (I like to think that's the right way to launch yourself - to risk loving someone else.)

Over the time, we realize this person incapacitates us in our dreams and projects, makes our lives bitter, detracts from us, makes us feel we aren't good enough and we allow it. Worse still ... we stayed years and years in that state of terrible living! ...

If you have the courage and maybe even a little luck, the day will come when you will say "no more". And so, with all the pieces which will have fallen on the road, you try to walk in the unknown and terrifying direction your life will now be. With the deepest fear you have ever felt (or perhaps stubbornness), you will grab your pieces and see if you should glue them again or develop thicker skin.

Whatever your decision, finally, as in an awakening from the coma of years, you will see yourself in the mirror and say to yourself: *"hello, thank you for being here again, I haven't seen you for a thousand years and I already missed you".*

If we are lucky enough to choose our partners, why do we settle for so little? ... why can't we accept when things stop being what they were and recognize that it's time to move forward?... the answer is simple "fear or comfort". Possibly both.

It's imperative that your life partner vibrate at the same frequency as you. By this I mean that, at least, he or she must be as clear as you are about what he/she wants from you and the world (together).

Because that person is the one who's going to live with you, the one who's going to make the decisions with you, the one who's going to influence the way you see the world every day. If you choose well it will be like winning lottery, but if you choose badly, you will be well fucked after a while. Didn't I already tell you that time is the only resource that really matters and the scarcest good that is granted to us? ...

Now let's talk about friends. Many times, family fulfills the role of friends, if you are very lucky. If not, then you have the opportunity to choose your friends according to your belief system, aspirations and intention. Many of us want to surround ourselves with friends who only serve a certain purpose, such as having them as potential customers in a business or project. Many others of us consider it valuable to have friends for parties.

I've found that many people have friends to avoid being alone with themselves, and those "friends" don't even like them. It doesn't matter if for you the meaning of friendship is directly related to "the possible contact for the possible business". If that's your choice, that's fine. Seen from a very practical perspective, you have chosen those people who serve a positive purpose in your life and that is ok, because you have decided to be better in business.

I can't tell you what kind of friends you should choose. That will depend on what you think about a friend is. Now, if you ask me what makes me choose one person over another to be my friend, the first thing I will tell you is I have become very demanding on this particular.

I have realized that a person whom I can consider "a friend" will have to have practically all these qualities:

- Respect for others ALWAYS.
- Black sense of humor
- Compassion with the weakness ones, with the less evolved human beings, with the ones who are in troubles
- Solidarity in all levels
- Love and respect for animals, children and seniors
- Self-love
- Clear ideas and strong points of views
- Courage to tell me when I screwing everything
- Emotional intelligence

- Don't make value judgments as if they were a superior entity who can make everything perfectly

I make this list and I smile, because so many lines are missing from the list that when I look at myself internally, I realize I ask a lot.

But in my favor, when I have a friend, I give the same to him/her, because that is balance; Because that's what truly successful relationships are and it's mandatory to offer the same in return. There's an old saying that says: *"tell me who you go with and I will tell you who you are".*

Why would you want to be with someone who's not as you would like to be? ... good question. Surrounding yourself with the right people at all times is almost mandatory. Because those correct people will be the ones who, in the end, will be with you to celebrate your achievements and to help you grow as an individual. And more importantly, those right people will be the ones to hug you when you think the world is going to end.

And I tell you something else, these kinds of people are very scarce goods that aren't available just around the corner. You can spend years looking for someone to participate and contribute positively in your life and possibly get one or two throughout it. That is why you must care for and love these people as if they were treasures. That is why you must be prepared to give your best, always and at all times, without selfishness, but without letting yourself be belittled.

My mother used to say there are two kind of people: *"those who come into your life as a lesson and those who stay in your life as a blessing"*. Now that you are on the road of investing in yourself, in your projects, in your dreams, you can´t afford dreaming about everyone wants to stay in your life. Possibly you don't even need them all. Learn how to filter. Learn how to let go of those who have been lessons. And every time you feel terribly sad because that person wasn't what you expected and he/she hurt you deeply, take a deep breath, close your eyes, thank him/her for the lesson and send him/her good vibes. In this way you will be in tune with the universe, learning what you should learn and preparing for the new person who arrives, who will surely be a blessing and will stay along the way.

CHAPTER 17
FEAR COMES IN ALL COLORS AND SHAPES

Talking about fear is sometimes scary. Fear is so evil that it starts like a little thing, and it grows inside you until you feel it in the bones, in the skin and even in the blood. Fear is so smart that it makes you feel that you need it, that you can live side by side with it and its only intention is making you cautious.

Fear knows where to hit you and how to make you feel worthless. Fear has the power to control everything you do, small or large, and to remind you on a daily basis, that your ideas aren't only crazy and difficult ideas, but also very stupid.

I have lived most of my life in fear. Since I was 10 years old and my father died in strange circumstances, I´ve been terrified that others will die, that they will abandon me, that they leave without saying me a word. Fear has paralyzed me from being the person I want to be and has made me waste 20 years living someone else's life, because I was never brave enough to live my own life as I always wanted.

So, if anyone knows about fear, that's me. Fear of being homeless, without money, without a partner, without savings. Fear of not being good enough, of not being pretty enough or smart enough to be loved by someone else. That was me, for sure!

And it's so paradoxical the way we live fear, that if you review my life, all those things used to scare me, already they happened to me because I lost my country and my house, I lost my money and my status , I lost my marriage and even, the respect for myself in several occasions; and all this, it only showed me, the only way to overcome fear is realizing that even having it, the things you fear most can happen to you and even so, you will continue to stand there.

Here I am, more prepared than ever to face the new project, the new person who crosses my life, the new financial or sentimental challenge. What happens is that now, although sometimes I am dying with all kinds of fears, in any case I throw myself headlong and I face whatever it's, because I am not going to give more power to my fears.

And that takes away their power and then I win the fight and I feel fantastic and a little stupid for having feared so much. Many people who have faced major catastrophes seem to agree that in 90% of cases, the hypothetical situation of fear we feel is even greater than the actual challenge or problem.

Because it's our imagination showing over and over again the most terrible scenario that sometimes will not even happen. And when it happens, everything bad we expected to happen was not so bad and we can go through that situation and we become stronger.

The first two years since I was alone, I spent all the time trying to find the way to completely annihilate the fear that I feel in front of many, but many things. Then, the last year, I realized that my fear and I must live some things together, but that doesn't mean we are the same entity. Now, we compete and I win.

When fear wants to overcome me, I find the strength and I jump headlong. Someone once told me that the best things in life often happen outside of our comfort zone. I always remember him with a smile, because it's true. Every time I get out of my comfort zone, I realize I have achieved a new step in my projects, that I have met more interesting people and that I have become a little wiser.

Now, my biggest fear is not trying something I really want to do. I get angry having that feeling I'm not going to be able to do something because of fear. I imagine myself in 10 years feeling like I lost another 10 years for not moving my ass and taking the risk.

I´m already know, there are different kind of risks and that balance is important. But at the same time, I am sure that in at least 80% of cases, what we want to do is to grow as human beings, as entrepreneurs, as a couple. But we stop doing it because we're afraid that will it go wrong and we don't want to fail. That's very stupid, not moving because you don't want to fail. Notice how, the fact of not moving is already, in itself, a failure.

Yes, fears come in all shapes and colors. And the only way not to be paralyzed is to force ourselves precisely to do what paralyzes us in the first place. It's putting ourselves little challenges every day, it's taking a step forward in what makes us to dream like children and we don't do it because we are terrified.

You don't have to do it all in one day or one week. One step at a time is all it takes to move forward. After a while, when you look back, you will realize you have advanced so much that you cannot even believe it. That will give you the confidence you need to continue dealing with your fears. Stop making up excuses! ... one step at a time! ...

CHAPTER 18
FORGIVE IT - FORGIVE HIM- FORGIVE THEM

I can never talk enough about how important forgiveness is. Living with some resentments is almost as wicked and terrible as fear. Sometimes forgiveness is all it takes to leave the past in the past and to have a wonderful life in the present. I know, forgiving is like a kick in the ass. But what other liberating options do we have to let go and move on? ... forgiveness is the best gift you can give yourself.

I know what it's like to be upset with yourself. I know what it's like to blame yourself for what you didn't say or what you didn't do when you should have. I know it may even take years to recognize you don't forgive yourself.

Humans like to hide resentments in the deeper level of their soul, trying to forget or hide them, as if somehow, they will magically disappear. But it's incredible how, after a few years, you realize that something happens and makes you relive what you tried to leave behind for years. Something very small, awaken everything that you once hid in the deepest hollow of your soul. And there comes again what hurt you and what will continue to hurt you, whether you like it or not.

There are people who remain stuck in terrible anger a lifetime. There are many who actually think their life has no meaning without their grudges. It's as if somehow the resentment they feel is what keeps them alive.

Maybe, even if you don't like to admit it, you hate your parents. You keep wondering why they were such terrible parents or why they didn't give you or why they didn't teach you what you needed to live better. I know many of these cases; so many.

For a few years, I felt a certain resentment towards my mother. Thank God I had the time before she died to tell her: *"I forgive you and please forgive me"*. By the time she died, despite the hollow left in my soul by her absence, I feel there were no unfinished business with her and I feel some peace in my heart.

Forgive your husband/wife, or your former partner or the one who takes your breath away but whom never knew how to love you. Forgive him/her because he/she, don´t know what he/she is missing, because he/she don´t know what you are willing to give for the relationship that they no longer have or never had.

Forgive him/her so that you can heal "the crooked leg that limps you" and that don´t let you be next to someone else, someone who will be there to give you happiness and support. It's the only way.

Forgive the friends who left you in the darkest moments of your life, those who judged you, those who spoke very bad about you and broke your heart. The world has more than 7 billion people, which makes it very likely you will find new enriching friends who want to walk with you and help you in your progress. Free those ones who have you in crisis, because I promise you, new people will come into your life, and they will leave you with a smile that you didn't even know you had.

CHAPTER 19
THERE ARE THREE TYPES OF PEOPLE

Everything I have learned in recent years has led me to this conclusion: There are (I think) three types of people. And it's somehow useful for me to catalog them like this, to be able to explain my point of view more clearly.

1) THE FATALISTS ONES

The fatalists are going to top my list because I think, they are the most common people; those are easier to find everywhere.

Fatalistic people are very well camouflaged and usually give you the impression they are collaborative, simple and friendly ones. They spend their lives trying to advise you because they think they know more than you about everything, because they have lived longer than you, and because they think their world view is much broader than yours.

They believe everything good and bad that happens, in some way, is determined by fate. They believe we are given a share of happiness or misery and there is a higher power that from the beginning, imposes on us what will be and what will not.

These people, although they often proclaim about "free will", aren´t sure about that. And it's so easy to verify it, because in the end resignation is their premise. Envy is their way of life.

These fatalistic people often never take action. They live and try to maintain their comfort zone at all costs and if something bad happens, they think they deserve it, and eventually, God can punish them and the situation can even get worse.

On the contrary, when something good happens to them, they say that "God protects the righteous" and thus, they feel as if the prize they were looking for has finally arrived. The paradox is that when they are in those terrible situations, they stay in them, waiting for the miracle that will get them out of there, but without lifting a finger to improve their condition. And since nothing lasts forever, sometimes they manage to get out halfway or get used to their new status quo.

2) THE SCARED ONES

I like and dislike these people at the same time. Because they are people who have potential for change when they decide to do it, when they finally "jump" into something else.

I used to be in this category. The scared ones are people who, even knowing that only by acting they will obtain the desired results, don´t do it for fear something will go wrong or for fear of what others will say.

The fear of ridicule or mockery, almost governs their lives. They know they are where they should no longer be or where they no longer need them. They know they aren´t happy, as happiness should be understood, but they are paralyzed, as if waiting for the perfect moment to reveal "the truth" to them.

The bad thing about this type of people is that over the years and knowing what they know, they begin to hold resentments, phobias and terrible fears, which end up getting sick their bodies and worse, that in the elderly, or even earlier, can produce a whole series of cancers and diseases.

As I said before, these people have potential, because at least they recognize what is wrong in their lives and eventually, they just need to develop the strength to take action and get out of there.

Everything will depend on how much they want their life to be different; how much they want to be happy and have the life of goals and dreams they always wanted. It's only there that frightened people begin to take control and overcome the level.

3) THE FREE ONES

These people are the product of the evolution that only blows, tragedies and heartbreak give. These people are the ones who, in the midst of the crisis, decided that they could no longer fall, because there is no more depth and the only way out is to go up.

These are the people who have understood everything good and bad that happens to

them in the "now" is directly proportional to the choices and decisions they made in the past. Those who
understand that the decisions they make today will define their future.

In this state, these people don´t come by chance. Here they come after a thousand battles, against themselves, against their environment, against their family, against their partner, against the chaos that controls their life. And it's that these people have learned not to settle for what they live.

They are those who take risks, those who in the midst of the crisis wonder what they can do to move forward and feel better. These people, who are sometimes scared to death, don´t allow fear to control their lives. One of the things I like most about free people is that they stopped caring about what other people think. That the fear they will say or the fear of making a fool of oneself is like a bad joke that makes them smile when they try something new. They are the ones that, despite not being perfect, are comfortable in their own skin and enjoy the process and the journey.

These people whom I admire so much and of whom I try to belong with each of my actions, are ultimately "THOSE THAT MAKE THINGS HAPPEN". The million-dollar question is: what kind of people do you want to be like? ... you still have time to make an intelligent decision! ...

CHAPTER 20
IT'S SIMPLE: "IF YOU DON'T BELIEVE IT, YOU'LL NOT ACHIEVE IT"

The power of visualization is a subject that I am passionate about. At first glance, many people could say it resembles fantasy. But it seems to me, as I have said on several occasions, that everything starts with a dream or an idea in your head. How could you start something, or create a new reality in your life, if you have never thought about it? ... are the aliens coming to insert an image or a solution in your head and that's it? ... (it's probable, but I still don't know anyone who was abducted by them).

1)   DREAM BIGGER

I don't remember who said this to me: "when you dream, you must do it big, because the chances are the universe will give you at least half of what you're dreaming of".

And if you're smart enough, you'll realize that if you dream just a little and you get a half, well, a half will be even less than a whole.

If you dare to dream big, and in the end, you also have a half, well, it'll always be a better half. So, here logic and common-sense rule. I don't think we just have to dream big to increase the probability in which we'll receive more. When I analyze this statement well, I don't even like it. I think we should dream about everything we want because it's simply our right, because it puts us on the right vibe and makes us feel we can conquer the world.

It happens to me that when I dream, for example, I have already sold a million copies of my books and look fabulous in my flower dress and high heels, my mood rises; And that day, I feel happier, livelier and more productive.

Sometimes when I'm having a bad day or something has happened and it has made me sad, I pause and visualize with something I really like and I want to do. It's like ... an essential oil.

I'm not saying, of course, that just dreaming will change the problem and when I return to reality, chaos or sadness will disappear as if by magic. But that moment has been a small gift I have given my soul, it makes me happy and helps me face problems. Period. I deserve it!

Generally, these moments where you visualize yourself and dream about things you want, with those situations that you want to attract to your life or with people you want to meet, leave you as if floating in a special vibe that many times becomes a reality. Because believe it or not, everything is connected.

You can call it metaphysics, witchcraft, or mirages. Call it what you want, but when you dream big, the universe conspires and somehow finds a way to give you just what you need.

2) HOW MUCH COST THE LIFE YOU WANT?

This is a question that has been going through my mind for months. At first glance it seems that we're talking about money, but this isn't necessarily the truth. Not everything in life can be bought, although some could say that everything has a price.

Maybe yes, everything has a price, but the currency, not in all cases, is money.

There are people who like to make lists and lists of the things they want and how much they cost. In this way, they know how much they have to produce in order to acquire what they want. They know how much effort they must put into their work to achieve their goal.

I particularly like to think the life I want is determined by other things, and that only with a good plan can it be achieved. And I mean to distribute the money and resources for the welfare of, for example, spending more time with my children or allowing myself more free time to sit down to write my ideas. It's all about to decide one thing or two, which bring you closer to what you need and want.

Because, sometimes what you need don´t exactly match what you want. So ... how much does the life you want cost? ... how much thrust? ... how much sacrifice? ... how much strength? ... how much forgiveness? ... how much freedom from real existential problems or imaginary? ... and also, why not, how much money? ...

3) LIST WHAT YOU WANT AND ASSIGN EACH ITEM A PRIORITY

Only very few people I know do this. My friend Monica is possibly my best reference. She has known for a long time what she wants, lists it, looks for what needs to be done and gets down to work. And of course, she assigns priority to what, according to her criteria, is the most important.

I love lists. I have them of all kinds: in the bathroom mirror to remind me that "I am enough" or that "today is going to be a great day", the ones on the wall and all the things I have to do every day to complete my work week; cell phones alarm ones which remind me of things that shouldn't forget even by chance, some for going to the market, the things I need to buy, the countries I want to travel to, and ... I even have lists of my dreamy shoes.

Doesn't matter what you want. Doesn't matter if it's material or immaterial, doesn't matter if it's equal to what others want or is even more important. You'll know what you want, what shakes you inside out, what takes your breath away. Make a list, give each item a priority, and plan to go after it.

4) INVESTIGATE - COPY – LEARN - REPEAT

As I always say and I will never be tired of repeating, we're in the perfect time to find the info and learn. Never before, (and I'm from the generation that grew up without computers, cell phones, and unlimited internet), we had been as close to the world as today, within a click.

I never stop being amazed by the amount of information, good and bad, to which we have access. It's like magic, it's like a super power, it's like traveling and learning without leaving your seat.

Research, in my opinion, is the basis of any entrepreneurship. I already said this before and I will not repeat myself again. What I will say is that we should "copy" as much as possible.

Obviously, I don´t mean to violate copyrights or as many companies in the world do, copy and sell their products as theirs, regardless of the damage they may do to other companies and people who have strived to create something new.

When I refer to "copying" I am basically talking about adopting and adapting, as far as possible, all those attitudes and mentalities that will surely make us more prosperous and better human beings. There are so many teachers and mentors at the click of a button!!! ... there are so many people to learn from anywhere, even in some corner of our city! ... not doing it would be stupid.

Learning is one of the most important skills in the evolution of the human being. It's basically what distinguishes us from animals, reasoning, and learning from one person to another. According to your learning, you'll stand out or sink. My advice is... "learn all you can; learn from everything; learn from everyone". Make learning one of your most important premises. I promise you'll see the results.

5) ASSIGN A DEADLINE TO YOUR PROJECTS

I used to think about projects and work hard for them. But I hadn't realized that every project must have a deadline date. Now, I have understood they should not only have a completion date, we must break them down into parts and assign them probable dates of scope and execution, in order to make them come true; to force us to achieve dates and obtain the expected results. This is not quantum science. The most productive and capable people are masters at "setting dates for their projects".

So now every time I start something, after planning and researching, I break my project down into tasks and assign these to a deliverable, a completion date. Now I advance with better achievements.

6) MEDITATE - PRAY - BE SILENT

There is something for everyone. There are those to whom prayer gives peace and tranquility because they feel connected with God, with "their God", with their divine essence. There are those who meditate to find within themselves the calm of a hectic and changing world. Through this practice, the human being "unlocks and restarts" from the inside out; and it's with this practice that, with the passage of time, people achieve the clarity they have always sought.

We live in a chaotic world of noise and interference. We live in a world in which all people certainly have an opinion about anything; in which everyone has a complaint, a suggestion. The worst of this case is that we listen to them and just a few things we take the time we need to listen to ourselves, to listen to what our soul, our supreme inner strength, is screaming at us.

Silence, praying or meditating is a smart tool that, far from boring you, it will show you there is much beyond the obvious. And no one wants to miss out on that super power that doesn't cost a penny, time, effort or planning. So ... go make silence, even for a few moments every day! ...

7)   PERSIST - RESIST - INSIST

Stubbornness ... a super power. Hold on to something you believe in and try it a thousand times despite the circumstances. The power to stay there when we want to give up, when we're tired to continue but internally, we know that it will work.

How many of us abandon an idea or project because it gets difficult? ... how many of us after a week of exercising like crazy ones, we abandon the gym because our legs or butt hurt? ... how many of us don´t have what it takes to resist and insist?...

It's easy to say, I know that. I've also had my episodes of "being on the verge of collapse" with the greatest desire to run away from everything.

And of course, in some of my most stupid moments I also did it and today I regret it like never before. But now, I can see the world through a better lens, I realize that when I want to give up because something has gotten complicated and I am very tired, what I need is to take a few moments to rest, but no to give up or to leave everything in half. It's very stupid to leave things halfway.

When you got there ... you only need the other half! ...

8) FEEL GRATEFUL

No matter what happens, feel grateful and say thanks. Be grateful for what you have in your life and fill your days. Be grateful for your terrible parents, for your unbearable children, for your husband's complaints, for the boring job you're involved in. Be grateful for the friends who have come and gone, for those who are still there, be thankful because your children have already finished the teenage stage, in which you wanted to throw them out the window, BE GRATEFUL FOR EVERYTHING.

Thanking for the good or easy things we have has no greater difficulty or merit, but still thanks for them. It takes a lot of courage to thank in the midst of the crisis for the lesson learned. It takes more strength than you think you have inside, to thank in the midst of the chaos and with tears streaming down your cheeks.

Remember that nothing in life remains the same, neither rigid nor permanent. Everything changes, everything moves, everything goes, everything comes back and everything improves. Thanks for it.

CHAPTER 21
THE GUARANTEED FORMULA FOR FAILURE

Do you want to know what it takes to have failure guaranteed? ... because I have already told you what I think can bring you to the right mindset you're looking for. Also, I told you how to start achieving the mindset to get anything you want to do in this life, from losing a few pounds to starting a business from scratch.

So, let's analyze it from the opposite perspective; from a different point of view. To begin, it would be pertinent to make a distinction between some concepts. Let's start with the definition of "a failure" and "a loser".

"A failure" is a temporary defeat of what is started or undertaken. And a loser is one who stays to live in failure. If we use elementary common sense, we'll know that "we all have failures" but "not all of us are losers".

Successful people have built their success on several failures. I like to call them "attempts". And is that my mother used to say that *"a loser never wins and a winner never gives up".* This is simply wonderful. But ... what do all the people who live in failure and end up being failed have in common? ... Let's analyze the product of my research. I have really meditated on this for a long time:

1)   NOT HAVE A WELL-DEFINED PURPOSE IN LIFE

Do you remember what you wanted to become when you were a little child? ... do you remember how simple it was to dream and be convinced that you would be great? ... do you remember not feeling any shame in telling everyone about it?... do you remember how organic you sounded that there was no hint of doubt? ...

I remember it, for sure. Since I was a little girl, I was very clear that I wanted to design. Of course, almost everyone thought they were very mediocre aspirations, because design in some Latin-American countries is more like a hobby than a prestigious job.

I could spend hours and hours designing collections for my Barbie dolls, for my Teddy bears, for my sister, for my classmates at school. I had a box of crayons with more than a thousand colors (I exaggerate a little bit, of course), and I took it with me everywhere.

I made paper clothes, I learned to knit when I was 7 years old, I used all the pieces of fabric my grandmother (who sewed) left around. I used to play with all the buttons were left of the clothes of a thousand years ago. I liked to think about what new outfits or models I would make to dress everyone in the house.

Of course, when I was between 7 and 12 years old, everyone was fascinated by the talent that I seemed to have. By the time I was a teenager, my mother and my family in general started pushing me toward a "more realistic option". And that more realistic option led me to the Faculty of Architecture, which filled me a lot, but did not make me entirely happy. By the time I was 17, I had already started working as a secretary in a construction company, not only to earn my own money, but to be able to learn with the best people in the field. They were all great to me and I learned a lot of things. But even a little part of me was limping.

When I got married and I had to move to my ex-husband's city, I left the college and I tried to start again in something else. I thought about the design career, but it sounded to me like an impossible mission.

It was an expensive career and so demanding that with two children, it would be crazy to jump into that "challenge". I remember my ex-husband saying: *"please Andreah, be more realistic"*.

With that he meant *"find yourself a career that gives you money and means something"*. So, I studied languages at the best university in my country and I don't remember a single day when it wasn't miserable. My dream was not to translate or interpret and pretend that with nice words in another language, we were going to change the world. Everyone's dream at the time was to translate or interpret for the United Nations. I only thought about dressing all the women who would read speeches, not translate them.

That's how fucked up my aspirations were: I was on the road, but not the right one. By the time my mother passed away and I was finishing my language degree, I had a kind of clarity, premonition, or quantum leap, which literally REQUIRED me to do something with my life that would make me happy and get me out of bed with a smile. Something to shake my butt like there's no tomorrow.

So, I made the decision to enroll in the most prestigious Institute of Design in my country, even if it cost me both eyes and a kidney to pay for. I would see how I would pay for it. I made my plan. My plan was so well planned that not only was I able to pay for my design degree, but I was the best in my class. That changed my life. With two small children, two dogs, a husband, a house to clean and no financial support, I set out for my destination with a well-defined plan. This is how it works.

Understand this for once: if you want to fail, I'm telling you again: DON'T MAKE A PLAN. Let yourself go through life as if you were floating in it. Maybe you're lucky enough and you'll get a nice place that gets you a decent smile.

2) NOT HAVING DISCIPLINE AND SELF-CONTROL

Wicked and unfair things will always happen to you, it happens to all of us. I don't think even Superman has been able to escape from that.

The "response" or "reaction" you have to face the situation, will determine the material you're made of. Leaving things to chance, because you don't have the motivation or the inner strength to continue in a moment of crisis, will be all you need to fail. You must be able to dominate yourself, before you want to dominate the situation. If you don't, prepare for outright failure after a few days or weeks.

3) POSTPONING EVERYTHING UNTIL YOU'RE MORE INTELLIGENT, HAVE MORE MONEY OR GET MORE SUPPORT FROM OTHERS.

Yes, you can wait, put off everything until your living conditions "improve", many people do. But, have you ever wondered ... what if the conditions never improve? ... what if the money you hope to have to get there, never comes to you? ... what if no one ever supports you? ... what if you don´t prepare or learn yourself, how will you be more competitive and intelligent? ... what will you do then? ...

If you're one of those who "wait", you're in the hole. Because the positive and good things that we all want in our life, we should not wait for them to happen. We're the masters of our destiny and we should go after everything we want in this life. We must make them happen.

In any other way, you can wait for them to happen, but you should wait in a good chair, because I assure you, the wait will be long.

4) BE NEGATIVE

Being positive or negative is a choice we make every day about anything. It's like choosing clothes, food or shoes for the day. It's preferring to think that everything can go wrong, instead of giving him the benefit of the doubt and giving you the chance to experience that everything can go well. Being negative will attract negative and even if any, mediocre results. Always happens. And when, despite being negative, good things happen to you, it means that you have just experienced a miracle, so stop being negative.

5) BE INTOLERANT

This is one of the worst qualities of a person, I think that intolerance is among those bad attitudes that take all the laurels. Intolerant people are terrible, because they are usually not well with themselves, with the environment or with other persons.

These bigots will always feel they have the right to criticize, question or sabotage all those who, according to their ideas, "don´t fit the box". Here I include xenophobes, homophobes and all those who reject others for being or thinking differently.

Do you want to go straight to failure? ... it's easy, be intolerant and close your mind. Not only you'll fail, but you'll learn nothing, and nothing from nobody.

6) EXTREME CAUTION

Just as there are people who start a project without a plan and end up in who knows what place, there are those who take such extreme precautions that they overstep the mark.

Extremes in any situation aren´t entirely recommended. Finding balance is ideal. If you take too many precautions and don't take risks from time to time; if you don't hear your instincts yelling at you from the inside that something should be done or something new might work, you're clearly not going to move forward.

7) LACK OF AUTHORITY. KNOW HOW TO SAY "NO"

How many times have we felt terrible about ourselves for saying yes, in favor of someone else, when we really wanted to say no? ... how many times have we felt used? ... even by people who say they love us?...

We must establish a posture that makes us happy and that consciously doesn't hurt others. But we must also remember that the first person in our lives is ourselves.

If we don't know how to give ourselves our place, we'll find us in infinite number of situations, in which we want to say no, but we end up saying yes, even to our detriment. Learn how to say "NO" is mandatory.

8) CHOOSING INSTANT GRATIFICATION BEFORE REWARDING FUTURE GOALS

This has surprised me. I used to be a person who gave myself little luxuries and gifts which worked as an instant gratification. In those moments I could tell myself: *"you need it or you deserve it"*. But probably, it never was true.

With these expenses it was impossible for me to save money to take my projects to the next level, as if waiting for something miraculous to happen and give me the money again.

In fact, I know many people, who fill their credit cards by buying things they don't need and they can't even afford, but that offer them instant gratification. If you want your project to fail, you know ... spend everything on things you don't need! ..

CHAPTER 22
EXTRATEGIC MENTAL CHANGES

1) LOVE WHAT YOU DO. LOVE IT SO MUCH.

Love will always be the most powerful force to create anything in this reality. I´ve always thought about this, because according to my experience, every time I´ve felt an immeasurable love, I´ve always gone further.

It's useless for you to embark on a project in which you don´t believe in. It's a waste of time to work on something that don´t inspire you enough to jump headlong for it and don't even think about anything else. If you don't madly love what you do, it might not be worth it and you should look for something else.

2) FIND UNTAPPED MARKETS

This would be ideal, don't you think? ...
Of course! ... who doesn´t want to take advantages of this kind? and position

themselves faster at the head of a market and have less competition? ...

Research, foresight and taking risks before others do, are the pillars of success in this area, both in personal and business aspects.

3) KNOW YOUR CLIENT – BE ABLE TO ADAPT TO CHANGING TIMES

More important than positioning yourself in a specific niche, you must discover the needs of your potential client. In my case, this has been a challenge from the beginning, because I´ve tried it in different countries, each country is different and the clients in each country have different needs.

Despite the fact that, with each attempt, I´ve felt I must start from scratch, over and over again; I´ve also learned that the main thing is to study your client, know their needs, offer them the quality they expect for the price they want and can pay. And mainly, don't forget to adapt to the changes, because the moment will come, when your client no longer needs your product. So, in that moment, you'll need to be able to reinvent yourself one more time.

4) LEARN FROM FAILURES. ANALYZE THEM OBJECTIVELY LEAVING THE FEELINGS ASIDE

Every time you fail at something, you should abstract yourself in such a way, that frustration, anger or sadness that you may feel, aren´t the filters with which you'll study the situation. You must know what went wrong and how you can do it again with better results. You should wait until you have a calm mind to investigate where you went wrong (even if it hurts) and how you can avoid doing it next time.

5) SURROUND YOURSELF WITH THE BEST

The way some companies operate in Latin-American countries always amazes me, over and over again. Perhaps that´s why in the end, we're still part of the so-called third world. And it's not this don´t happen in more developed countries; it's that it seems the smartest and most successful have the premise of surrounding themselves with those who are the best in their area and paying them equally, to keep them motivated and in that state of high productivity.

In Latin America, it's often preferred to hire the cheapest and not the best qualified employees. It happens to me, that I´ve lost contracts because my product is better and therefore, the cost is a little higher. People want to take advantage of the profit without considering the effort, the genius, the quality which is offered to them. If you want not only to position yourself at the head of something, but you want your profits to be proportional in the end, you'll always have to surround yourself with the best in each area of the business. It's the smartest way of achieving more in less time.

Analyze millionaires and creators of globally successful companies such as Bill Gates or Steve Jobs or even Mr. Jack Ma who created the Alibaba Group mega business consortium. Do you think they alone could have done everything they have achieved? ... well NO. Intelligence also consists in knowing you need others as good as you to advance, to grow and even to compete. So, every time you add someone to your team, in your project, in your dreams, think well if that person seriously works in the same line in which you're going on.

Think carefully about whether that person is willing to give their best to make your dream come true, and have the decency to pay him/her just enough for it and reach agreements that benefit the team. At the end, it's a joint effort that must be rewarded. You have to have an abundance mentality.

6) SUCCESS DON'T COME OVERNIGHT

This seems to have been repeated to exhaustion. We have heard it for so long that we're no longer paying attention and still hope the results of our efforts will come immediately.
So, we get frustrated and quit everything. Think about this well and continue. Stay there, trying it from another perspective if you think what you're doing is not working. Be aware that everything is a process and

over time you'll reach your goals. Don't give up.

7) BE GENEROUS WITH OTHERS

Every time I think about this, I keep remembering my parents. They were influential people in their environment at the time. Heirs, so to speak, of what the surname already brought before birth.

However, one of the qualities I always remember from my father was his simplicity in dealing with others. Always at the helm, he had the gift and the courtesy to remember the name of every employee, secretary, foreman, and even of all the people who were in even lower positions in the hierarchical organization chart of his work team.

When the royalties of the year came, when a harvest produced more than expected, when the money raised was more than planned, my father never forgot all those who contributed to achieve it. I remember him because I used to go with him to the farm, to his meetings with those who asked to speak with him to seek help with their needs.

When my father got somewhere, he was literally like a rock star. It was only until I was growing up that I realized it was due to the generosity with which he always treated those who were outside their status or social condition.

My mother on her side was always ready to help, advise, share. My mother was a descendant of people who escape from war in Spain and the Franco dictatorship. It was very clear to her since she was a child, that everything you have you can lose it in a second and that only the relationships you have been able to build with others, it's what will keep you on your feet.

Solidarity for my mother was the most important quality in a human being. Now, after everything I lived in my own country, I can understand what solidarity really means. Venezuelan people are living in their own flesh a despotic government which took everything in a bad way.

8) LIFE IS NOT FAIR ... LIVE WITH THAT!

Life is not fair. I always said it, and it was only until I heard once Bill Gates saying it in an interview, it was I realized I wasn't so crazy to think or feel it. Life is just the path that leads you to evolution, perhaps Buddhists would say.

And in this way, thousands of things will happen to you that must happen to you so you can learn. Probably, this is the way Universe is telling you how to value people or things, or situations.

Perhaps this is the meaning of life: knowing how to resist the thousands of things that will leave you crying on your knees.

Live with it! ... and please move your ass in the right direction. Staying on your knees crying is not going to make you progress, for sure.

CHAPTER 23
NEGOTIATION - ADAPTABILITY - EMPATHY
(ESSENTIAL QUALITIES TO LEARN)

Many of us believe "NEGOTIATION skill" means more like the ability to influence and/or deceive others. If you ask some people in your environment, you'll be surprised with the answers you're going to get. Sometimes the word "negotiation" sounds a little aggressive.

It's incredible that most people simply assume negotiation is the ability to defraud the "helpless poor people you meet along the way".

In his book "*The 7 Habits of Highly Effective People*", Stephen Covey points out there are 6 trading models and that "Win-Win" (perhaps the best known) is just one of them. For the author, the combinations between the two possible winners of a negotiation is more a philosophy of life than a business technique and that is why not everyone practices it properly.

It's no secret to anyone we all want to win, even if winning means putting ourselves first, even ahead people we love. It doesn't matter if the loser is right; we continue with the crazy desire to win the negotiation even if we cheat.

We can see in these negotiation models we'll always be inclined to those who only provide us with a benefit: **1) Win/Win, 2) Win/Lose, 3) Lose/Win, 4) Lose/Lose, 5) Win and 6) No deal.**

In the first case and my favorite par excellence "Win/Win" is the goal always. I am not comfortable with any other. I know that it cannot always be achieved, because as the saying goes, "it takes two tango".

I've learned, by losing a lot, that Win/Win means rising above individual interest, joining forces and seeking the best shared benefit. For this reason, to dance "this tango", you need two involved. Not everyone would agree to letting the other win.

The other two points are pretty obvious: 2) Win/Lose and 3) Lose/Win. The second one only demonstrates the use of authority to make a profit; the pleasure of knowing that somehow, you're in a position of power. Winning you and knowing that you lost gives you the evil pleasure of feeling superior.

"Losing/Winning" seems to me a delicate point in its analysis, because rather than bothering the other you prefer to surrender and let him/her win, in a search to please the winner at any cost. This model seems more dangerous to me than the previous one, because in the end and although they don´t agree, these people give up what they believe in order not to create conflicts. These are the victims of life, those who in some way will never go far, because their self-esteem is so battered and non-existent, they will never win for fear of taking control even of the negotiation.

Point 4) Losing/Losing is nothing other than the philosophy that if you lose, then the other one will also lose. It's like revenge. It doesn't matter if you don't get any of this, "if I'm screwed, you're going to be screwed too".

This is the philosophy that usually prevails in large-scale conflicts, such as wars, for example. It seems to me this point is also a form of consolation: since nobody wins, we console ourselves thinking we're on equal terms.

When we speak of "I Win" (form of negotiation number 5), the purest selfishness prevails here. It's no longer evens a matter of wishing the other to lose. Here we simply have the goal of winning at all costs, without even thinking about who could lose. There's not much more to explain when excessive selfishness is the protagonist of the equation.

Point 6: "No deal" refers to those occasions in which neither of the two parts in conflict "give in" and delay the negotiation as long as possible, until they see who surrenders first and who wins by "abandonment".

This usually happens in many commercial cases, however, it can also be seen in family fights, where unconsciously, when we say "we'll not negotiate", we secretly wait for the other one to surrender; And so, we should not even feel guilty for having won, because from the outset, we didn't even want to win.

Only until we internalize that the negotiation must serve the sole purpose of giving value to the other, of making them and their ideas feel important, and on the way to making the two parties benefit from the agreement, we'll not understand the great power that it has. healthy and responsible negotiation.

And this don't only apply to business. I would venture to say that it applies to a greater extent with the people we love. Let us remember the art of negotiation "is not the art of manipulation". It could be, for sure, but in the end, the price is always paid, whether we understand it or not.

When we talk about ADAPTABILITY, firstly, we must understand that nothing remains the same forever. Everything will change, whether you like it or not. And this applies to all.

Let us remember that famous quote by Darwin which said: *"... the species that will survive would not be the most intelligent ones, but those that best adapt to change ..."*

In this case, the same could be said, and with this, practically everything is said already. Wanting to keep all situations frozen in time isn't possible. The only thing that perhaps is possible is we're the ones who continue to be as stubborn about this idea over time. And even then, something will happen that will kick our asses and make us move, whether we want to or not. Going with the times is the only smart move we can make if we want to survive. And more importantly, if we want to overcome any situation.

Don't pretend that because you think you're doing the right thing everything is going to stay as it's. Bad things also happen to good people. It's about modifying behaviors, strategies, looking for new resources and everything that helps us to be in tune with the changes.

I'm not talking about resignation; I'm not talking about getting used to living in shit because that's just what you can do when change comes and it's not favorable for you or your environment. It's knowing how to stop, how to understand, how to make a plan and looking how to execute it, get up and continue: "with your face up and towards the wind". This is having an attitude and adaptability, that is, being resilient.

And what about EMPATHY? ... Empathy is a beautiful quality only very few of us have. It's such a great, innate, or learned ability in which you get yourself in the other´s shoes, even if you do it only for a few seconds.

Empathy is knowing how to observe everything and everyone without judging, as to know what it's about or where we're standing. It's being able to identify what others feel, what they want, what they dream about, what is difficult for them, how they are prepared for their environment.

Empathy is beautiful because it makes us better people, more kind and compassionate ourselves and of course, much better prepared for challenges and success.

So, think carefully before judging others: your rival or your friend. Your partner, your son or whoever. Try to get yourself in his/her shoes for once, not to justify him/her when he/she does something wrong, but to understand him/her and to understand his/her motivation whatever they are.

I am sure this will expand your mind when it comes to making better decisions. At the end of the day, isn't the objective? ... to make the best decisions which guarantee a good negotiation, so that both parties are winning and happy, right? ...

Let's go a little further... if this explanation seems too simplistic to you. A person who don´t feel threatened, who has benefited from an agreement and who feels that his/her idea has been considered, will be a happy person. Happy people don´t go through life gossiping about other´s lives, sabotaging others, criticizing or seeking conflict.

Imagine for a moment, you don't have to watch your back or being expecting in a couple of days, someone is going to screw your project with conflicts, because someone did something or said something about it. Imagine for a moment everyone is in harmony wanting to help you reach your goal, because they are happy and feel they have contributed "to the cause". Believe me, this is Win/Win! ...

CHAPTER 24
ENJOY YOURSELF...
THIS IS YOUR JOURNEY!

This will be the last chapter of this book and I could not close it without telling you I am REALLY grateful you allowed yourself to get here. Because even though many of the things I told you sound very ridiculous or as if I was kicking your ass myself, you were better than that, and allowed yourself to learn from my experience.

This book has taken me several months of learning and data collection. This book could summarize all the strategies I've learned since I was left alone. When I look back, maybe three years ago, I realize how much I've advanced and how much I've grown as a human being, but above all, as an empowered woman.

I've learned to combat my fears and choose my battles, to take advantage of my strengths and to work in those ones which sometimes make me feel weak and stupid. I've met people who have enriched my life to unimaginable levels. They have also broken my heart into a thousand pieces, it's true, but almost no one escapes from that.

Breaking into a thousand pieces, depending on how you look at that, can mean being stranded on the road, or it can be the turning point towards something much better and stronger is going to come for you.

So, I've no regrets. This path which will start for you now, can only be a path where you, as the protagonist of your life, will not only be the most important person in the world, but also, you have become a wiser person and better prepared for what is going to come, good or bad.

By now, you must have rethought many things you want to change and many others you want to do. I am very pleased if I've been able to help you with my experience. Since I started with this book, my intention was clear: to give you a little bit of me, so your path would be more bearable and happier.

I am sure destiny brings the right people in your life, to learn or to enjoy. If we're very lucky, they will love us madly and support us in our wildest and most exciting dreams, but we'll not know if we don't take risks.

This new chapter that begins today will be your life, not mine anymore. I´ve my own trip. You're planning yours now, if you haven't already mapped it out yet. Maybe this book woke up the last little parts that fell asleep out there and should wake up.

Perhaps this book shook you to the ground. Anything this book has done for you is profit. And it's all yours: it's "your profit". It makes me a little sensitive to know this chapter of my life is closed, but I cannot lie to you ... I jump from the emotion of thinking about a new one is opening, and perhaps ... I am going to meet my life partner, my co-star, who is going to give color to my mornings and nights and with whom I hope to reach a very old woman surrounded by grandchildren, dogs, flowers, trees and much, but much love.

Another book will come, with the help of God and my own will. I'm not going to stay in the uncertainty of whether I´ve something else to communicate. Having knowledge only forces you to share it and many don´t do it because they simply don´t care. That will not be our case, because I am sure that with much or little, you have learned from everything we have discussed in this book, you'll surely share it with others. That's what it's about, connecting, being, sharing and loving in all possible directions. That is, as I see it, the purpose of life.

Thank you so much!
I wish your live is so intense as you deserve it and not boring at all! ...

(This book was written in Santa Fe de Bogotá, Colombia. I´ve been living here again for 8 months now)